Joy and Peace

A Poetic Devotional
by
Marcia Kay Carlson

with photos by Ron Huffman

Printed in the United States of America

First Printing, 2017

ISBN 978-1-9795033-1-0

Dedicated to

Jorie Gulbranson
who radiates Joy

and

Cheri McDonald
who personifies Peace

They are both women of God who have richly blessed my life
for many years as friends, mentors, encouragers, prayer warriors,
and radiant models of Christlikeness. Truly,
"I thank my God in all my remembrance of you"!
(Philippians 1:3)

Many Thanks to:

My children, Rebecca, Scott and Melanie, who fill my life with joy every day through their unique personalities, delightful gifts, and excellent characters.

My husband, Drew, who has brought unconditional love, needed balance, and multifaceted peace to my life for over twenty-five years!

My father, Ron Huffman, who is always ready to encourage and assist me in any way he can, and who took all these beautiful pictures and generously permitted me to use them.

My mother, Carol Huffman, who is my ever-available friend, supporter, mentor, prayer warrior and sounding board extraordinaire!

May the God of hope fill you with all joy and peace in believing,
so that by the power of the Holy Spirit you may abound in hope.
(Romans 15:13)

Table of Contents

Know that the LORD, he is God! It is he who made us, and we are his; we are his people, and the sheep of his pasture. *(Psalm 100:3)*

Can a woman forget her nursing child, that she should have no compassion on the son of her womb? Even these may forget, yet I will not forget you. Behold, I have engraved you on the palms of my hands; your walls are continually before me. *(Isaiah 49:15-16)*

If I take the wings of the morning and dwell in the uttermost parts of the sea, even there your hand shall lead me, and your right hand shall hold me. *(Psalm 139:9-10)*

"For the mountains may depart and the hills be removed, but my steadfast love shall not depart from you, and my covenant of peace shall not be removed," says the LORD, who has compassion on you. *(Isaiah 54:10)*

But when the fullness of time had come, God sent forth his Son, born of woman, born under the law, to redeem those who were under the law, so that we might receive adoption as sons. *(Galatians 4:4-5)*

See also—Isaiah 43:1-4, Isaiah 26:3-4, Lamentations 3:22-23, Psalm 18:19, Psalm 100:5

Divine Possession

"I'm God: the LORD, for My name's I AM,
And you are My sheep, My beloved lamb.
I formed you right in your mother's womb.
I care for you now, leaving fear no room.

"So, you are Mine, I have called you by name—
Now doubly you're Mine, for you then became
A child redeemed from all sin and death
To live just for Me with your every breath.

"Created, ransomed—as both, you're Mine,
But there is still more to My grand design:
The LORD your God—I am yours, as well;
In Me, you will find boundless treasures dwell.

"My thoughts are yours, and I can't forget
You as My dear child: for it's you I've set
Before My eyes, and I did engrave
You on My own hands that reach out to save.

"My hands are yours: they will guide and lead,
And they will provide you with all you need.
My loving arms will surround, enfold,
And with My right hand I shall you uphold.

"My presence is yours, for there's not a place
That cannot be reached by My warm embrace.
Through waters, rivers, through fire, alarm,
I'm still with you, so they cannot harm.

"My peace is yours, for you trust in Me,
And I am your Rock for eternity.
Though hills and mountains may run away,
My covenant of peace will surely stay.

"My mercies are yours—they will never end.
Each morning your cares I perceive and tend.
I'll save, for you're My delight, you see.
You've trusted in Me, so your foes must flee.

"My love is yours; it will never cease.
Forever enduring, it can't decrease.
My faithfulness will outlast each age
And grant you new gifts as you face each stage.

"Then, lastly, even My Son is yours;
He shattered sin's wall—opened heaven's doors.
I gave my best, O My precious one;
You've all that is Mine, and you're now My son!"

And Moses said to the people, "Fear not, stand firm, and see the salvation of the LORD, which he will work for you today. For the Egyptians whom you see today, you shall never see again. The LORD will fight for you, and you have only to be silent." *(Exodus 14:13-14)*

[A]nd [the priest] shall say to them, "Hear, O Israel, today you are drawing near for battle against your enemies: let not your heart faint. Do not fear or panic or be in dread of them, for the LORD your God is he who goes with you to fight for you against your enemies, to give you the victory." *(Deuteronomy 20:3-4)*

"Thus says the LORD to you, 'Do not be afraid and do not be dismayed at this great horde, for the battle is not yours but God's…You will not need to fight in this battle. Stand firm, hold your position, and see the salvation of the LORD on your behalf, O Judah and Jerusalem.' Do not be afraid and do not be dismayed. Tomorrow go out against them, and the LORD will be with you." *(II Chronicles 20:15b, 17)*

"Are not two sparrows sold for a penny? And not one of them will fall to the ground apart from your Father. But even the hairs of your head are all numbered. Fear not; therefore, you are of more value than many sparrows." *(Matthew 10:29-31)*

See also—Psalm 103:14, Genesis 15:1, Isaiah 41:10, Luke 2:10-11, Romans 8:15, Revelation 1:17-18

Blessed Reassurance

Our great God truly knows our frame;
He remembers He formed us from dust.
So, He gently puts forth His claim:
"My dear child, I am here; simply trust."

The refrain of God's holy Word
Is "Fear not, and don't be thus afraid."
Yet, our panic stays undeterred;
We ignore our Lord's offer of aid.

God, appearing to Abram, said:
"Do not fear, because I am your shield."
Abram followed just where God led;
He had faith though God's plan was concealed.

God sent Moses to bring release,
Yet Egyptians still barred Israel's way:
"O, fear not; just stand firm; hold your peace,
For the Lord fights for you now today."

Then, God's people encountered war
With great armies outnumbering their own,
So the priests spoke to underscore
God would not let them be overthrown:

"Don't give way to your fear or dread,
And refuse to be fainting in heart.
It's the Lord who will fight instead;
Victory's sure when your God takes your part!"

Joshua's mentor advised, "Be strong
And take courage; do not be distressed.
God won't leave you your whole life long.
He is with you; assured, you can rest."

Then, a prophet proclaimed, "This fight
Is not yours; it is God's; do not flee.
Do not fear this great horde tonight,
For, tomorrow, salvation you'll see."

With his God as his light and strength,
Israel's psalmist found no one to fear.
We can face even strife's great length,
For wherever we are, God is here.

Once again, comes the cry, "Fear not,"
As the Lord through Isaiah declares,
"You are never an afterthought.
You are Mine, for I made you; I care!

"I, the Lord who made all, am He
Who will help and give strength—worry not!
You'll remain still unharmed, you'll see,
Though with floods and with flame you have fought."

Lowly shepherds one night were told,
"Now, fear not, for a Savior's been born.
This good news of great joy, behold,
Is for all: yes, the weak and the worn."

"Not one sparrow could fall to earth,
And your Father not know," Jesus said.
"Have no fear; you're of greater worth,
And God numbers the hairs of your head."

Paul explained, we're not slaves to fear,
Since the war for our souls has been won.
When we cry, "Abba! Father!" He'll hear,
For we've now been adopted as sons!

"So, fear not, I'm the first and last,"
Says the Christ, who now lives though He died.
And when death and all fears are past,
Then, in heaven, we'll live at His side!

From Old Testament to the New—
Our first day to our darkest of night—
All God's promises have proved true,
For God's presence makes fear take to flight.

Behold, I am doing a new thing; now it springs forth, do you not perceive it? I will make a way in the wilderness and rivers in the desert. *(Isaiah 43:19)*

Therefore, if anyone is in Christ, he is a new creation. The old has passed away; behold, the new has come. *(II Corinthians 5:17)*

And I will give them one heart, and a new spirit I will put within them. I will remove the heart of stone from their flesh and give them a heart of flesh, that they may walk in my statutes and keep my rules and obey them. And they shall be my people, and I will be their God. *(Ezekiel 11:19-20)*

The steadfast love of the LORD never ceases; his mercies never come to an end; they are new every morning; great is your faithfulness. *(Lamentations 3:22-23)*

Then I saw a new heaven and a new earth, for the first heaven and the first earth had passed away, and the sea was no more…And he who was seated on the throne said, "Behold, I am making all things new." *(Revelation 21:1, 5a)*

See also—Philippians 1:6, Jeremiah 31:31-33, Luke 22:20, John 13:34-35, Ephesians 4:20-24

Receiving Renewal

Start dieting, exercise—lose weight,
And banish the foods that I overate.
Next, pick up and clean up, organize.
Devotions and prayer time revitalize.

The New Year is here; let go remorse.
Resolve now to alter my life's old course.
Is there any change that I have missed?
And what does God say when He sees my list?

"My child, you're not bound by what you've done,
For I will complete all that I've begun.
Creation does groan in fallen state,
But I still do reign, and I still create.

"For I am the One who makes new things:
Like paths in the wilderness, desert springs.
Delivering you through all your days,
I give you new songs so that you can praise.

"The Law left My people bound, afraid,
And so, a new covenant I have made.
It's drawn once for all in Jesus' blood—
No sin can withstand that pure, cleansing flood.

"In Christ, you're a new creation, too.
The old's passed away; what has come is new.
You have a new spirit and new heart.
You're now consecrated and set apart.

"Upon your new heart, I wrote My law;
And this new commandment for you I draw:
As Christ has loved you, so love each man,
And, thus, you'll fulfill all My law and plan.

"Now, flippantly, by the world you're told:
'Bring in all the new and take out the old.'
'Put off the old self and don the new':
This I say, for sin no more masters you.

"You have My new life each day, each year.
Still looking ahead with unease and fear?
You're safe in My boundless love and care;
Each time that you wake, see new mercies there.

"This old, fallen world will pass away:
New heaven and earth—dawn of endless day.
Stand strong, now, on what I've promised you:
Behold, I will surely make all things new!"

Blessed are those whose way is blameless, who walk in the law of the LORD! Blessed are those who keep his testimonies, who seek him with their whole heart, who also do no wrong, but walk in his ways! *(Psalm 119:1-3)*

This Book of the Law shall not depart from your mouth, but you shall meditate on it day and night, so that you may be careful to do according to all that is written in it. For then you will make your way prosperous, and then you will have good success. *(Joshua 1:8)*

Blessed is everyone who fears the LORD, who walks in his ways! You shall eat the fruit of the labor of your hands; you shall be blessed, and it shall be well with you. *(Psalm 128:1-2)*

Oh, taste and see that the LORD is good! Blessed is the man who takes refuge in him! *(Psalm 34:8)*

The Crucial Contrast

(adapted from Psalm 1:1-4, Jeremiah 17:5-8)

The psalmist sang, "That man will be blessed
Who does not walk as the wicked suggest,
Nor does he stand where sinners do walk,
Nor does he sit where the scoffers will talk.
But in God's law, he takes great delight,
And on it he meditates day and night.

"He's like a tree that's planted by streams
That yields its fruit as its harvest time deems—
A tree whose leaves won't wither, because
He prospers, too, in all things that he does.
The wicked aren't like that, rather they
Are just like chaff that the wind drives away."

The prophet held, "That man will be cursed
Whose strength is flesh, who puts trust in man first,
Whose heart is turned away from His God.
He's like a shrub in the desert's dry sod.
His eyes will see no good from that sand;
He'll dwell alone in that parched, salty land.

"But blessed is he who trusts in the LORD.
He's like a tree grown where water is poured,
That sends out roots to where the streams run
And does not fear the strong heat of the sun;
The year of drought it faces in peace,
For come what may, it bears fruit without cease."

Two ways of life, two ends juxtaposed:
Effects and cause by God's love are disclosed.
To grow strong, bear fruit: trust God, love His law;
Don't trust and crave only what your eyes saw.
For, though man has no source of life on his own,
The water of life ever flows from God's throne!

And my God will supply every need of yours according to his riches in glory in Christ Jesus.

(Philippians 4:19)

The young lions suffer want and hunger; but those who seek the LORD lack no good thing.

(Psalm 34:10)

For thus said the Lord GOD, the Holy One of Israel, "In returning and rest you shall be saved; in quietness and in trust shall be your strength." *(Isaiah 30:15)*

Be appalled, O heavens, at this; be shocked, be utterly desolate, declares the LORD, for my people have committed two evils: they have forsaken me, the fountain of living waters, and hewed out cisterns for themselves, broken cisterns that can hold no water. *(Jeremiah 2:12-13)*

"These things I have spoken to you, that my joy may be in you, and that your joy may be full."

(John 15:11)

I say to the LORD, "You are my Lord; I have no good apart from you." *(Psalm 16:2)*

See also—Matthew 11:28,30; Romans 8:28-29, Psalm 40:8, II Corinthians 12:9-10, Psalm 13:5-6

A Believer's Journey Toward Faith

As a child, I accepted Your Son;
Your good news I did truly believe.
Yet distrust still remained in my heart;
So much truth I had failed to receive.

"The great weight of Your rules is too much—
Lord, I cannot do everything right!"
You invited, *"Child, come unto Me!*
My yoke's easy; My burden is light."

But I doubted that Your will was best,
For my own will was not being done.
You declared, *"I work all for your good,*
Since your best is to be like My Son."

Always anxious, I thought that I must
Ever serve You to prove I had worth.
But You whispered, *"Be still; know I'm God,*
And I will be exalted on earth."

I excused, "I need comfort! I'm stressed!
Can't help eating much more than I should."
You then pled, *"Find your refuge in Me!*
Taste and see, and you'll find I am good."

Still, I argued, "I need what I want!
I must have all the pleasure it brings."
So, You promised, *"I'll give all you need;*
Those who seek Me will lack no good thing."

"I can't meet life's demands, Lord," I cried;
"My own skills aren't enough to get through."
"Child, My strength is fulfilled when you're weak,
And My grace is sufficient for you."

Tried so hard, yet I failed, then lost hope.
"God, don't leave! I so long for the grave."
"It's in quiet and trust that's your strength.
Just repent and then rest, and I'll save."

"You're the Fount of living waters, my Lord,
Yet, with sin, that true life I forsake."
You assert, "I will give you much more
Than the bare, broken cisterns you make."

"Jesus taught so that I might have joy—
The same joy with which His heart was filled."
"That real joy you can have which was His
Is to do just the things I have willed."

"Father, why did despair last so long?
And why couldn't I hear what You said?"
"So you'd trust, not in self, but in Me;
I'm the God who can raise up the dead."

"You're 'the God of all comfort,' so when
I look elsewhere for help, it's not there."
"I have comforted you all this time
So that you can give others My care."

"In this world, I'll face challenges still,
And I know I'll still fall, but I'll rise."
"When you feel that you sit in the dark,
That's when I'll be a light for your eyes."

"Your great pleasure is not in my strength;
I don't have to do all things just right."
"Those who hope in My merciful love
Give Me pleasure and are My delight."

"So, I'll boast about how I am weak,
That Christ's power may rest upon me."
"True contentment can come with distress;
When you're weak, then you're strong: that's the key."

"I'll let go of anxiety's weight.
With thanksgiving, I'll bring my request."
"Then, My peace that you can't understand
Guards your heart and your mind—gives you rest."

"Body fails, yet my spirit's renewed—
Won't lose heart nor give in to despair."
"I will use this light pain which soon ends
To bring glory beyond all compare."

"I will say to the Lord, 'You're my Lord,
And I've nothing that's good besides You.'
I will trust in Your love and rejoice,
For You've brought and You will bring me through!"

He heals the brokenhearted and binds up their wounds. *(Psalm 147:3)*

Then they cried to the LORD in their trouble, and he delivered them from their distress. He brought them out of darkness and the shadow of death, and burst their bonds apart. *(Psalm 107:13-14)*

Sing for joy, O heavens, and exult, O earth; break forth, O mountains, into singing! For the LORD has comforted his people and will have compassion on his afflicted. *(Isaiah 49:13)*

"Blessed are those who mourn, for they shall be comforted." *(Matthew 5:4)*

Now may our Lord Jesus Christ himself, and God our Father, who loved us and gave us eternal comfort and good hope through grace, comfort your hearts and establish them in every good work and word. *(II Thessalonians 2:16-17)*

The Christ's Commission

(adapted from Isaiah 61:1-3)

Isaiah saw the Messiah's true call
In the words that God's Servant would speak to all—
"The Lord God's Spirit is on Me, I say,
For the LORD has anointed Me in this way:

"For all the meek, I've good news to present,
And to bind up the brokenhearted I'm sent.
And I proclaim that the captives are free;
For the prison is opened—I hold the key!

"Now is the acceptable year of the LORD
When His favor and blessings will be outpoured.
The day of vengeance from God, yes, is near,
But My comfort for all those who mourn is here:

"To grant to those who in Zion now mourn—
To give beauty for ashes, and thus adorn;
With oil of joy, I'll end mourning's next phase
And exchange heavy spirits for garb of praise.

"I do all this so that they might be named
Trees of righteousness: thus, My truth is proclaimed.
This planting made by the LORD will abide;
He'll be seen in His people and glorified."

Then, when the Christ in the synagogue preached,
For this part of Isaiah's long scroll He reached.
He'd come to do all that God spoke and willed,
So Christ said, "Now this Scripture has been fulfilled."

The risen Christ gives His Church now His call:
"Go ye therefore and make disciples of all."
We have His Spirit and Good News to say;
And His comfort we spread, for we know the Way!

The LORD your God is in your midst, a mighty one who will save; he will rejoice over you with gladness; he will quiet you by his love; he will exult over you with loud singing.

(Zephaniah 3:17)

Let the word of Christ dwell in you richly, teaching and admonishing one another in all wisdom, singing psalms and hymns and spiritual songs, with thankfulness in your hearts to God. And whatever you do, in word or deed, do everything in the name of the Lord Jesus, giving thanks to God the Father through him.

(Colossians 3:16-17)

But if we walk in the light, as he is in the light, we have fellowship with one another, and the blood of Jesus his Son cleanses us from all sin…If we confess our sins, he is faithful and just to forgive us our sins and to cleanse us from all unrighteousness.

(I John 1:7, 9)

He who dwells in the shelter of the Most High will abide in the shadow of the Almighty.

(Psalm 91:1)

Wait for the LORD; be strong, and let your heart take courage; wait for the LORD!   *(Psalm 27:14)*

See also—Colossians 3:12-15, Galatians 5:22-23, Isaiah 30:15, Isaiah 40:31, Psalm 91:14-16

Delight, Direction, and Deliverance

(for a friend, based on her favorite scriptures)

"I'm the mighty One who guards your ways.
I've rejoiced as you have sung My praise.
But, My child, just pause and listen, too,
As with joy I'm singing over you!

"Come to Me, My child, My little lamb;
For your Shepherd is the great I AM.
So you shall not want: you're in My will.
You'll enjoy green pastures, waters still.

"Then, My faithful child, you'll bend your ear
As I teach the path of righteous fear.
You desire life—to see good days?
Speak the truth and seek for peaceful ways.

"And put on—My dear and chosen one—
The compassion and kindness of My Son.
Now, to bear with others is how you live.
You're forgiven, so you must forgive.

"You're to clothe yourself with love, which ties
All in harmony that purifies.
Let the peace of Christ control your heart
And be thankful, as one called apart.

"Let Christ's word in you, then, richly dwell
And with wisdom teach—exhort as well.
You'll sing psalms and hymns, the Spirit's songs,
And your heart will thank Me all day long.

"So whatever you do, or say, or sing,
Thus, in Jesus' name do everything,
Giving thanks to Me, your God, through Him,
Whether things in life look bright or dim.

"For when hope is dim, I am your light—
Your salvation from both foes and fright.
I'm the stronghold of each life I made,
So you need not ever be afraid.

"It's your trust in Me that blocks out fear.
Set your mind on Me; then peace appears.
You can trust in Me forevermore—
The eternal Rock is your guarantor.

"You are blessed through trust, My daughter dear:
You are like a tree with water near.
Neither heat nor drought cause you dismay;
Your green leaves and fruit My works display.

"For the Spirit's fruit is love, joy, peace;
And then patience, kindness will increase.
Finally, faithful, gentle, self-controlled,
You'll fulfill the Law—its truth uphold.

"Even though you're with My Spirit filled,
There are times you fail at what I've willed.
But I'm just and faithful when you confess
To forgive and cleanse unrighteousness.

"Thus, no condemnation's now allowed—
You're in Christ, with righteousness endowed.
And I work all things for good, you know,
For I've called you Mine from long ago.

"So, I'll save, when you repent and rest,
And in quiet trust, with strength you're blest.
I'm the shelter you can dwell inside;
In My shadow, then, you will abide.

"To renew your strength, just wait for Me;
You will soar with eagles' wings, you'll see.
Then you will not tire as you run your race,
And you will not faint as you walk by grace.

"Even if you walk where death draws near,
I will go with you, so you won't fear.
For no evil can withstand My rod,
And My staff's marked out the paths you've trod.

"You hold fast to Me and know My name,
So I'll answer you when you exclaim.
I'll deliver, rescue, honor you,
And I'll satisfy your whole life through.

"Finally, wait for Me—it won't be long.
Let your heart take courage, and be strong.
For My goodness and love shall fill your days;
In My house you'll forever sing My praise!"

He will tend his flock like a shepherd; he will gather the lambs in his arms; he will carry them in his bosom, and gently lead those that are with young. *(Isaiah 40:11)*

"I am the good shepherd. The good shepherd lays down his life for the sheep." *(John 10:11)*

His divine power has granted to us all things that pertain to life and godliness, through the knowledge of him who called us to his own glory and excellence, by which he has granted to us his precious and very great promises, so that through them you may become partakers of the divine nature, having escaped from the corruption that is in the world because of sinful desire. *(II Peter 1:3-4)*

When the perishable puts on the imperishable, and the mortal puts on immortality, then shall come to pass the saying that is written: "Death is swallowed up in victory." "O death, where is your victory? O death, where is your sting?" *(I Corinthians 15:54-55)*

"And I will ask the Father, and he will give you another Helper, to be with you forever, even the Spirit of truth, whom the world cannot receive, because it neither sees him nor knows him. You know him, for he dwells with you and will be in you." *(John 14:16-17)*

See also—Exodus 3:14-15, John 7:37-39, Hebrews 4:15-16, John 6:35, Revelation 5:11-12

16

Sheltered by the Shepherd

(outline based on Psalm 23)

God's covenant name is "the LORD, I AM,"
And He's my shepherd who carries each lamb.
He seeks all the lost and retrieves the strayed
And tends His flock: all the people He made.

And Christ's the good shepherd, whose life laid down
Redeems His sheep—even gives them a crown.
I'm carried through life and then on through death
To heaven bought with the Shepherd's last breath.

So, how could I want? Every good was won,
Secured for me by the blood of the Son.
For body, soul, spirit, I've all I need:
No circumstance His provision exceeds.

Green pastures, still waters—then, what are these?
His Word and Spirit my weakness to ease.
With words sweet to taste—living water, too,
He'll fill me up, and my strength He'll renew.

Delivered from sin, now my soul's restored
And finds its rest in the yoke of my Lord.
He makes His yoke easy; His burden's light.
I'll come and learn from Him all that is right.

He leads me along as He goes before
On paths of righteousness—straight to His door.
I'm ushered right in through Christ's name alone:
By grace, I come to the foot of God's throne.

No evil can harm me, for God is here;
In life or death, then, I won't ever fear.
For death's just a shadow; I'll feel no sting.
It has no power; Christ holds its key ring!

And You're truly with me, Immanuel.
Your Spirit comforts as in me You dwell.
Your rod You will use to fight back my foes.
Your staff extracts me from danger I chose.

You act as my host; thus, you care for me:
You fix a table as full as it's free.
With wine that's Your blood—living bread, your flesh,
You grant to me Your new life ever fresh.

My head is now blessed by Your Spirit's oil;
He helps and counsels through all of my toil.
My joy in my Lord overflows my cup,
For at Your table each day I will sup.

Your goodness and mercy and steadfast love
My whole life long I won't find the end of.
They've followed me everywhere You have led,
Entwined through life as You've woven each thread.

Since Christ has now gone to prepare a place,
Then, in God's house, when I've finished my race,
Forever I'll dwell where the Shepherd reigns
Victoriously as the Lamb that was slain.

"For as the rain and the snow come down from heaven and do not return there but water the earth, making it bring forth and sprout, giving seed to the sower and bread to the eater, so shall my word be that goes out from my mouth; it shall not return to me empty, but it shall accomplish that which I purpose, and shall succeed in the thing for which I sent it." *(Isaiah 55:10-11)*

"[N]o weapon that is fashioned against you shall succeed, and you shall confute every tongue that rises against you in judgment. This is the heritage of the servants of the LORD and their vindication from me, declares the LORD." *(Isaiah 54:17)*

And so, from the day we heard, we have not ceased to pray for you, asking that you may be filled with the knowledge of his will in all spiritual wisdom and understanding, so as to walk in a manner worthy of the Lord, fully pleasing to him, bearing fruit in every good work and increasing in the knowledge of God. May you be strengthened with all power, according to his glorious might, for all endurance and patience with joy, giving thanks to the Father, who has qualified you to share in the inheritance of the saints in light. *(Colossians 1:9-12)*

See also—Psalm 40:1-4, Psalm 148, Psalm 121, Psalm 23, Isaiah 43:1-2, Psalm 143:8

In the Fortress of the Father's Favor

(for a friend, based on her favorite scriptures)

"Lord, I knew You not when I was young;
I was hurt by acts and words that stung.
Yet my waiting You did not deny—
You inclined to me and heard my cry.

"From destruction's pit You drew me out
And dissolved the miry clay of doubt.
Then upon a rock You set my feet:
Made my steps secure, my joy complete."

*"Now, My child, you seek My kingdom first;
It's My righteousness for which you thirst.
Thus, obedient child, I hear you plead,
And I add to you all things you need."*

"So, my God, I sing the new song You gave;
It's a song of praise to You who save:
'Praise the LORD! O, praise Him in the heights!
Praise Him, sun and moon and stars of night!

'Praise Him, highest heavens, waters, land—
God created each by His command.
Let all praise His name and its great worth,
For His majesty's above the earth.'"

*"As I promised, scores did see and fear
And put trust in Me when they did hear
You sing praise and testify of Me,
For I sent you forth to set men free.*

*"Thus, at home or on the mission field,
Know My Word shall ever harvest yield.
It accomplishes the goal I meant
And succeeds in that for which it's sent.*

*"Hence, no weapon forged to harm prevails;
You'll refute each tongue's accusing tales.
This, the heritage My servants share;
I will vindicate, the LORD declares."*

"Oh, my Father, I lift up my eyes,
For my help comes from beyond the skies—
From the LORD who does both make and keep.
I am safe: my Keeper does not sleep."

*"Child, indeed you're safe by night and day;
I will keep you from all evil's sway.
See, I work all things for good to you,
For I've called you, and you love Me, too.*

*"I'm your shepherd, so I meet each need;
In green pastures, by still pools I lead.
You are mine, and I have called you by name.
You will not be hurt by flood or flame."*

"Let me hear Your steadfast love each morn;
Lord, in You I trust, so peace is born.
Let me know how I should choose my way,
For to you I lift my soul each day."

*"I restore your soul, lead you to take
All the righteous paths for My name's sake.
You're My honored guest before your foes.
I anoint your head; your cup o'erflows."*

"Lord, I've learned to trust with every breath.
Though I walk through vales and shades of death,
I will fear no evil—You're with me,
And Your rod and staff are comfort's key."

*"Child, I'm pleased you trust and intercede.
All My sheep you love in word and deed.
As you pray for them, you, too, I fill
With the knowledge of My perfect will.*

*"You've the Spirit's wisdom, wield His sword;
Thus, your walk is worthy of your Lord.
And I'm fully pleased with your pursuit,
For in each good work, you bear My fruit.*

*"You will know Me more each day and hour.
I will strengthen you with all My pow'r.
So, according to My glorious might,
You'll endure with peace and joy life's night."*

"As I trust You, Lord, I find I'm blest.
I have come to You and found my rest.
Now, You've good to show me all my days.
Then, I'll dwell in Your house in ceaseless praise."

Why are you cast down, O my soul, and why are you in turmoil within me? Hope in God; for I shall again praise him, my salvation and my God. *(Psalm 42:11)*

Remember my affliction and my wanderings, the wormwood and the gall! My soul continually remembers it and is bowed down within me. But this I call to mind, and therefore I have hope: The steadfast love of the LORD never ceases; his mercies never come to an end; they are new every morning; great is your faithfulness. "The LORD is my portion," says my soul, "therefore I will hope in him." *(Lamentations 3:19-24)*

I shall not die, but I shall live, and recount the deeds of the LORD. The LORD has disciplined me severely, but he has not given me over to death. *(Psalm 118:17-18)*

If the LORD had not been my help, my soul would soon have lived in the land of silence. When I thought, "My foot slips," your steadfast love, O LORD, held me up. When the cares of my heart are many, your consolations cheer my soul. *(Psalm 94:17-19)*

You make known to me the path of life; in your presence there is fullness of joy; at your right hand are pleasures forevermore. *(Psalm 16:11)*

THE POINT OF PUNCTUATION

Capital letter: start of a name,
Start of a sentence—a new life came
Into the world, by God's hand was created.
Given a family: God's love demonstrated.

At first, my life was a question mark:
"What is the sun, and why is night dark?"
I asked things of the world; it also asked me,
"How far will you go, and just who will you be?"

Exclamation points as child, through teens;
Such strong feelings—sure what it all means!
Got straight A's in school, so assured of success;
Then boyfriend's proposal, and my starry, "Yes!"

At once, life centered 'round ampersand.
I filled the blank: was half of "Drew & --."
A few years to adjust, then came another:
Smiles & tears, joy & grief as "wife & mother."

But, the commas of Bipolar II
Punctuated my adult life through:
A bit up, then way down—took decades to learn
How to moderate high, survive crash and burn.

Along the way, marks of quotation:
Mother's advice and inspiration,
Drew's patience and love, but God's Word, most of all:
"Trust in Me and have hope; I'll catch when you fall."

I grieved the omissions—ellipses…
Paralyzing guilt from my disease.
So much could not do for my family and friends…
And the cycles keep coming—it never ends…

Now, more questions: "How is this okay?
How can I survive another day?
Why can't I be normal and busy, like 'They'?
Doesn't God care? How can He want it this way?"

Longed for the period to end my life.
Life, and I, didn't seem worth the strife.
Unbearable pain with what seemed no escape:
I could not come to terms with life's crooked shape.

Then dawned the semi-colon of hope;
Grasped this knot at the end of my rope.
My sentence *could* end, but goes on to new things;
My song is not done; the Creator still sings!

Death is a colon when in God's time;
He is the Poet: I, just the rhyme.
Door to eternity, not grave that swallows:
Death's colon just leads to the joy that follows!

On a clock's face, colon, too, is a sign:
Hours' and minutes' dividing line.
So death separates all my days, months and years
From forever-life: free of pain, death and tears!

Semi-colon now; colon to come:
How should I march? How beats my life's drum?
I know now, though questions and tears punctuate,
God's love underlines all, and He's never late!

I have been crucified with Christ. It is no longer I who live, but Christ who lives in me. And the life I now live in the flesh I live by faith in the Son of God, who loved me and gave himself for me.

(Galatians 2:20)

Or do you not know that your body is a temple of the Holy Spirit within you, whom you have from God? You are not your own, for you were bought with a price. So glorify God in your body.

(I Corinthians 6:19-20)

Then Jesus told his disciples, "If anyone would come after me, let him deny himself and take up his cross and follow me. For whoever would save his life will lose it, but whoever loses his life for my sake will find it."

(Matthew 16:24-25)

Therefore, since we are surrounded by so great a cloud of witnesses, let us also lay aside every weight, and sin which clings so closely, and let us run with endurance the race that is set before us, looking to Jesus, the founder and perfecter of our faith, who for the joy that was set before him endured the cross, despising the shame, and is seated at the right hand of the throne of God.

(Hebrews 12:1-2)

See also—Genesis 5:24, John 4:34, Colossians 3:23-24, Matthew 5:16, John 15:5

The Words of New Life

Some scriptures have long stood out to me
As meaning more than I could yet see:
Could not live them out through all my strife,
But knew they should be true of my life.

They felt like a door on which to knock,
Or keys that had not turned in my lock.
Now wisdom has come through trial's guise;
I hope to look at them through fresh eyes:

First, Enoch had walked so close with God:
God took him home—right off of earth's sod.
I long so to walk with God each day
That He's my Home, not what's made of clay.

Like Paul, I've been crucified with Christ;
I'll live my life as one sacrificed.
Christ lives in me now—by faith I live:
No longer I, but life that God gives!

The Holy Spirit's temple I am;
I'm not my own, but bought by the Lamb.
I'll glorify God, who's on my throne.
The vital key: I'm not now my own!

I'll follow my Lord—avoid true loss:
Deny myself and take up my cross.
For I will just lose what I would take,
But I will find what I give for His sake.

"My food is to do God's will," Christ said,
"I complete God's work as My daily bread."
Like Him, when I do what God has willed,
I'll know my needs have all been fulfilled.

I work, not for men, but for the Lord;
From Him is my eternal reward.
So, serving the Lord as set apart,
I do all tasks with all of my heart.

I must let God's light in me so shine:
They'll see my works as good, but not mine.
They'll glorify God, who reigns above—
I live to show His truth and His love.

How do I receive the life that shines?
I must abide—a branch in the Vine.
Abiding in Christ, much fruit I'll bear;
Apart from Him—no fruit anywhere!

What's fruit? What's God's will? Ever rejoice!
In all things, make thanksgiving my choice;
And come to my God for cares' release,
For He commands I pray without cease.

Surrounded by saints—that cloud so great,
I must now lay aside every weight;
The sin which so closely clings I'll rout
And run with patience the race that's marked out.

Now, "looking to Jesus" is my theme.
He bore the cross for the joy: to redeem.
He's seated with God—Victorious Son,
So I run a race that's already won!

I sought the LORD, and he answered me and delivered me from all my fears.   *(Psalm 34:4)*

The fear of the LORD is the beginning of wisdom; all those who practice it have a good understanding. His praise endures forever!   *(Psalm 111:10)*

Oh, fear the LORD, you his saints, for those who fear him have no lack!   *(Psalm 34:9)*

He fulfills the desire of those who fear him; he also hears their cry and saves them.   *(Psalm 145:19)*

The fear of the LORD leads to life, and whoever has it rests satisfied; he will not be visited by harm.   *(Proverbs 19:23)*

Behold, the eye of the LORD is on those who fear him, on those who hope in his steadfast love, that he may deliver their soul from death and keep them alive in famine.   *(Psalm 33:18-19)*

Oh, how abundant is your goodness, which you have stored up for those who fear you and worked for those who take refuge in you, in the sight of the children of mankind!   *(Psalm 31:19)*

See also—Psalm 103:17-18, Deuteronomy 5:29, Proverbs 1:7, Psalm 147:10-11, Proverbs 14:27

Reverent Response

"Fear not, says your God"—comfort wrapped in command:
A rule we can't miss if God's Word we have scanned.
But then, we are told of "the fear of the Lord,"
Which, too, is required and will bring a reward.

Now, David sought God and was saved from his fears,
Yet those who fear God are the ones that He hears.
So, what is this fear that we're taught to maintain?
And what does God say that we thereby will gain?

The ones who fear God take delight in His law
And choose to obey, for they hold Him in awe.
They know His love fashioned the covenant He made
With rules drawn to prosper them—not to upbraid.

Thus, fearing the Lord, they give ear to His call,
Revering their God as the One above all.
Then, trusting God's word, they take refuge in Him
And hope in His love, though they face what looks grim.

This "fear of the Lord" is where wisdom begins,
With knowledge and insight to keep us from sin.
As well, it makes way for our Father to bless;
It pleases Him more than we ever could guess.

On those who fear God He will not turn His back;
He gives what they need, so there's nothing they lack.
Still more, the Lord God will fulfill their desire,
And they'll not be harmed though dark threats should transpire.

To those who fear God, He will show loving care.
His eye's fixed on them to set free from despair.
For them, steadfast love from the Lord will not cease,
With blessings stored up which abound and increase.

So, fearing the Lord is the way we respond
To God, the Most High, in this world and beyond.
Then, safe in His hands, we don't fear earthly strife,
For fear of the Lord is a fountain of life!

But Joseph said to [his brothers], "…As for you, you meant evil against me, but God meant it for good, to bring it about that many people should be kept alive, as they are today."

(Genesis 50:19a, 20)

For the LORD God is a sun and shield; the LORD bestows favor and honor. No good thing does he withhold from those who walk uprightly. *(Psalm 84:11)*

Therefore, my beloved brothers, be steadfast, immovable, always abounding in the work of the Lord, knowing that in the Lord your labor is not in vain. *(I Corinthians 15:58)*

Now to him who is able to keep you from stumbling and to present you blameless before the presence of his glory with great joy, to the only God, our Savior, through Jesus Christ our Lord, be glory, majesty, dominion, and authority, before all time and now and forever. Amen.

(Jude 24-25)

See also—Hebrews 11:6, Jeremiah 9:23-24, Philippians 3:7-10, 13-14; Psalm 16:11

Prepared by Pain for Works that Remain

(for a pastor, based on his favorite scriptures)

"Lord, I was marked at such a young age:
Tragedy seemed to fill my life's stage."
"But, child, I marked you blameless, upright,
To be a man of peace and of light.

"The enemy hurled that cruel event,
But all that reached you was the good I'd sent.
Looking back, you see I've used those pains
To impart new life and break old chains."

"I know, for those whose hearts turn to You,
You work all things so good will ensue.
I also know, for sheep in your fold,
There's no good thing that You would withhold."

"Child, I am pleased with this faith I hear;
This is the faith that will draw you near—
You trust that I AM, though you can't see;
You know I reward those who seek Me.

"So I gave you strength and made you wise,
But there's just one thing that you must prize:
That You know and understand My worth—
How with justice and love I rule the earth."

"Lord, indeed, there is one thing I ask;
It will be my most beloved task:
All of my days in Your house to dwell
And of Your beauty to learn and tell."

"This boon that you ask comes with a cost.
With Christ, you will seek and save the lost.
Like Him, dear child, you'll count all things loss,
Deny yourself, and take up your cross."

"Yes, I'll share Christ's sufferings while I've breath,
So I may be like Him in His death.
Then I'll know His resurrection might—
Since to know Christ more is my delight."

"You share the love that caused Me to give
My only Son so the world could live.
Those who trust in Him are saved from sin,
So I send you out their souls to win.

"Therefore, go into all creation—
Make disciples in every nation.
I send you to baptize in My Name,
And what I teach you, teach them the same.

"But do not fret over loads you bear;
Give thanks to Me and lift up your prayer.
Then into My hands your cares release
And find you're secure in perfect peace.

"And when you're tired, just wait upon Me;
I'll give new strength, and weakness will flee.
You'll fly over heights where eagles soar.
When others must quit, you'll run some more.

"Thus you'll remain unmoved and steadfast,
Fruitful in Kingdom work that will last.
You know your work is what I ordain;
Your labor, then, is not done in vain."

"My ministry, Lord, has spanned long years;
You've carried me through both smiles and tears.
The past I'll forget, then press on, like Paul—
My eyes on the prize of Your upward call.

"Father, You've shown me the path of life:
Fullness of joy in the midst of strife.
Your presence brings joy in this dark land,
And pleasures abound at Your right hand.

"For I am sure neither life nor death,
The present's choice, nor the coming breath,
The depths down below, nor heights above
Could separate me from Your great love."

"I preserve you now from stumbling's shame.
I'll present you then washed clean of blame
Before My glory with great delight.
And Christ comes soon to dispel earth's night!

"Now, you are marked with the praise I give,
Not just Above, but while you yet live:
Come, enter into the joy you've won—
My faithful servant, well done, well done!"

The people who walked in darkness have seen a great light; those who dwelt in a land of deep darkness, on them has light shined. *(Isaiah 9:2)*

In him was life, and the life was the light of men. The light shines in the darkness, and the darkness has not overcome it. *(John 1:4-5)*

For God, who said, "Let light shine out of darkness," has shone in our hearts to give the light of the knowledge of the glory of God in the face of Jesus Christ. *(II Corinthians 4:6)*

Again Jesus spoke to them, saying, "I am the light of the world. Whoever follows me will not walk in darkness, but will have the light of life." *(John 8:12)*

Rejoice not over me, O my enemy; when I fall, I shall rise; when I sit in darkness, the LORD will be a light to me. *(Micah 7:8)*

See also—Psalm 139:11-12, I Peter 2:9, I John 1:5, Isaiah 60:1-2, Isaiah 42:16

Love Song for the Light

Can I write of you, Father, as my light?
Depression's returned like descending night.
You've assured me, though, that You'll lead me through,
For night is as bright as the day to you.

In the dark, I'd walked—could not understand:
Eternally safe, but dwelt still in dark land.
Now, I've seen the light that I'd known was there:
The light of Your Son which evicts despair.

As John said, "In Him was true life," and then
"The life that You sent was the light of men."
When You shine His light in my world that's dark,
The darkness has not overcome Its spark.

At time's birth, You said, "Let the light shine in."
The Fall, though, began the long night of sin.
Now, You've shone in hearts with the light of grace:
The knowledge of Glory in Jesus' face.

Though Your Son was slain for my sin once for all,
I need Your light daily because of the Fall.
Now, delivered once from sin's cost and sway,
I'm called into light each and every day.

You're my light and salvation, so what's to fear?
In You is no darkness at all, we hear.
Never let me fear what is in your will—
The light of Your love guards my pathway still.

In that path, I'll follow Your Only Son:
The Light of the world, who light's victory won.
Likewise, You, Lord God, are a sun and shield:
Your light's no less real when by clouds concealed.

Your new call to me is "Arise, and shine!"
My light has now come, for my light is Thine.
Thus, Your Glory's here, and when clouds intervene,
I'll know that, not by, but upon me it's seen.

When depression comes now to paralyze,
I'll hold to Your Word: "When I fall, I'll rise.
When I sit, and darkness seems all I see,
It's then that You, Lord, are a light to me."

So, I'll trust in You as I take each breath,
Through nights filled with trouble or pain or death.
For, I need not fear any future night:
All darkness before me You'll turn to light!

Commit your work to the LORD, and your plans will be established. *(Proverbs 16:3)*

If any of you lacks wisdom, let him ask God, who gives generously to all without reproach, and it will be given him. *(James 1:5)*

In the cover of your presence you hide [those who fear you] from the plots of men; you store them in your shelter from the strife of tongues. *(Psalm 31:20)*

Charm is deceitful, and beauty is vain, but a woman who fears the LORD is to be praised. *(Proverbs 31:30)*

And God is able to make all grace abound to you, so that having all sufficiency in all things at all times, you may abound in every good work. *(II Corinthians 9:8)*

For we are his workmanship, created in Christ Jesus for good works, which God prepared beforehand, that we should walk in them. *(Ephesians 2:10)*

See also—Matthew 11:28, Philippians 4:13, 19; Psalm 138:8, 3; Colossians 3:23-24, Psalm 121:7-8

Provisions for Providers

(For the Women in the Workplace Ministry, Westminster Chapel, Bellevue, WA)

"Have you worked so long to secure your place
Just to fight every day to maintain?
Have your goals outrun your most rapid pace?
Is 'all work and no play' your refrain?

"Come to Me, My daughter, who labor so;
Bring your burden, and I'll give you rest.
All your cares and struggles I see and know;
For each need, I will give what is best.

"Does your life feel like a huge juggling act:
Work and friends, family care, home to run?
It's My strength that keeps parts and whole intact;
You can do all these things through My Son.

"Do you doubt that you've truly heard My call?
Do you fear you're not in the right place?
I fulfill My purpose for you in all;
I will guide as you're seeking My face.

"Do you have a boss who's unskilled, unkind?
I'm your Boss—work for Me as your Lord.
Work with all your heart as for Me, then find
That from Me you'll receive your reward.

"Or, are you the boss with ten things to do
All at once? The demands never cease!
On the day you call, I will answer you,
And the strength of your soul I'll increase.

"Are there projects, schedules that may fall flat?
Do you fear your work won't make the grade?
Child, commit your work unto Me, so that
I'll establish the plans you have made.

"Does it seem like nothing you do will last—
Like it's futile, or surely mundane?
Know your work's for Me—thus, you'll stand steadfast,
And your labor cannot be in vain.

"Do you thirst for wisdom to face life's tests?
Here's the promise I made for this need:
Ask of Me—I love to make rich bequests,
And I'll give wisdom freely indeed.

"Have you wounds from censure and parting shots?
Can you never forget what you've heard?
See, My presence hides you from human plots;
I'm your shelter from strife caused by words.

"Do you feel unsafe in your job or with kin?
I will guard as you walk through each door.
I'll protect when you go out or come in
From now on and forevermore!

"Do you ask yourself if they'll know you're Mine?
Yes, My glory they'll see upon you.
Now your light has come, you'll arise and shine
Into darkness My light will pierce through.

"Is your need to advance causing you distress?
Is there more that should be in your charge?
Know My hand's with you: that indeed, I'll bless,
And your borders I'll ever enlarge.

"Do you always seek for more beauty keys?
Must you meet every standard that's raised?
Know that charm's deceptive and beauty flees;
It's the woman who fears Me that's praised.

"Do you tire of being 'provider' still?
Have you found your own strength's not sufficed?
Every need of yours My supply will fill
With My riches in glory in Christ.

"Now, I give to you all-abundant grace:
All you need at all times I have shared.
You're My workmanship: till you see My face,
You'll abound in good works I've prepared!"

Trust in the LORD with all your heart, and do not lean on your own understanding. In all your ways acknowledge him, and he will make straight your paths. *(Proverbs 3:5-6)*

Praise the LORD! Blessed is the man who fears the LORD, who greatly delights in his commandments! ...He is not afraid of bad news; his heart is firm, trusting in the LORD. His heart is steady; he will not be afraid, until he looks in triumph on his adversaries. *(Psalm 112:1, 7-8)*

I have stored up your word in my heart, that I might not sin against you. *(Psalm 119:11)*

Delight yourself in the LORD, and he will give you the desires of your heart. *(Psalm 37:4)*

[M]ay the Lord make you increase and abound in love for one another and for all, as we do for you, so that he may establish your hearts blameless in holiness before our God and Father, at the coming of our Lord Jesus with all his saints. *(I Thessalonians 3:12-13)*

See also—I Samuel 16:7, Psalm 108:1, Matthew 22:37-38, Deuteronomy 31:6, Psalm 73:26

A Heart not Whole, but Holy

(for Mary Reeve)

"My child, you may have a faulty heart:
It is weak—beats too slow or too fast.
But since you are Mine, that's not the part
Of yourself that is key and will last.

"The heart in your chest may be diseased,
But My eye's on your spiritual core,
And when I see that, I am well-pleased
With your heart as it loves more and more.

"My Word has described the heart that's Mine,
Which you've let Me develop in you.
I love how you've lived by My design
With a heart that is steadfast and true.

"Fulfilling My great and first command,
You do love Me with all of your heart.
Then, all of your heart does trust My hand,
And it follows the course that I chart.

"Because of such trust, your heart won't fear,
Though huge armies and battles you face.
You fear only Me, so triumph's near;
Your heart's firm, putting Me in first place.

"You've stored up My Word within your heart,
So you'll not commit sin but do right.
Your heart's true desires I will impart,
Since in Me you have taken delight.

"I've shone in your heart, so you have known
Of My glory through Jesus' great name.
Thus, when He returns to take His throne,
I'll establish your heart without blame.

"My child pure in heart, you're of great worth.
I am with you, whatever's in store.
The strength of your heart I am on earth,
And your portion I'll be evermore!"

33

Cast your burden on the LORD, and he will sustain you; he will never permit the righteous to be moved.
(Psalm 55:22)

Though the fig tree should not blossom, nor fruit be on the vines, the produce of the olive fail and the fields yield no food, the flock be cut off from the fold and there be no herd in the stalls, yet I will rejoice in the LORD; I will take joy in the God of my salvation. GOD, the Lord, is my strength; he makes my feet like the deer's; he makes me tread on my high places.
(Habakkuk 3:17-19)

"Everyone then who hears these words of mine and does them will be like a wise man who built his house on the rock. And the rain fell, and the floods came, and the winds blew and beat on that house, but it did not fall, because it had been founded on the rock."
(Matthew 7:24-25)

Count it all joy, my brothers, when you meet trials of various kinds, for you know that the testing of your faith produces steadfastness. And let steadfastness have its full effect, that you may be perfect and complete, lacking in nothing.
(James 1:2-4)

See also-Genesis 50:20, Joshua 1:9, Psalm 42:11, Isaiah 26:3-4, John 14:27, Philippians 4:6-7,11-13

Reaching for the Rock

What all is required so I'll feel "okay"?
Must my day and my plans go just my own way,
With health that is good—well-rested, well-fed—
And with others to say, "Well-done" and "Well-said"?

Must mirrors reflect all I want to see,
And my past—must it seem to be mistake-free?
Ahead, must the future seem rosy bright?
If that's true, then my peace is nowhere in sight!

How much of me is under outside control?
Is it just a small part, or most of the whole?
Am I all depressed, or else, all uptight
Unless everything's going fine and just right?

Such bondage! Did God ordain this for me?
For this prison of mine, does He hold the key?
In fact, Jesus died so I'd be set free:
Free on earth, and not just in heaven, you see.

God wrote a huge book so I could be taught
Of His servants whose peace He lovingly bought.
Their words and their lives are songs that still sing
Of a peace that withstands what hardships will bring.

At peace, years of prison Joseph endured,
For he knew this great truth—by faith was assured:
"Though others have done what evil they could,
I will not, thus, be harmed; God meant it for good."

As Joshua faced God's plan to invade,
Moses charged, "Do not fear or be now dismayed.
Be strong and courageous; victory's in store,
For the Lord is with you, and He goes before."

The psalmist could see his soul was downcast
But perceived that his turmoil wasn't to last.
He hoped in his God, not earthly reward.
"God's my Savior," he said, "so I'll praise the Lord."

King David advised, "Cast burdens and pain
All upon the Lord God, and He will sustain.
Your trust is in God, so nothing can shake:
You will never be moved, for God won't forsake."

Isaiah declared, "God keeps him in peace
Whose whole mind stays on God, who trusts without cease.
That mind is at rest—that trust is secure,
For our God is the Rock; He'll ever endure."

Through famine and strife, Habakkuk's faith soared;
He rejoiced, not in wealth, but in his true Lord.
With God as his strength, with feet like a deer,
He could tread on the heights with nothing to fear.

Then, Jesus proclaimed, "Your feet must now stand
On the rock of my word, and not on loose sand.
The peace of this world requires all in place,
But the peace that I give rests only on grace."

Christ said we could have true peace now in Him,
Though affliction's dread cup be full to the brim:
"This world will attempt to tear you apart,
But now I've overcome the world, so take heart."

Paul urged, "Worry not about anything,
But instead, send your pleas to God on prayer's wing.
God's peace that's beyond what you comprehend
Will then guard heart and mind, as Christ did intend."

Through prison and pain, Paul knew what peace meant:
"I have learned at all times to be most content.
In plenty or need, I've found the true key:
I can do all these things, since Christ strengthens me."

In James, though, the highest standard we find:
"You must count it all joy through trials of all kinds.
These tests of your faith will keep you on track;
They will make you complete, mature, with no lack."

"Trust God, live by faith, and, thus, be content"—
It's the message with which the Bible was sent.
I'm weak; how can I live here as God willed?
Jesus gave what I need: I'm now Spirit-filled!

And, thus, not this world's but the Spirit's control
Will equip me to say, "It's well with my soul."
External things' hold will ever decrease,
For the Spirit's first fruit is love, joy, and peace!

Upon you I have leaned from before my birth; you are he who took me from my mother's womb. My praise is continually of you. *(Psalm 71:6)*

For my father and mother have forsaken me, but the LORD will take me in. *(Psalm 27:10)*

For you did not receive the spirit of slavery to fall back into fear, but you have received the Spirit of adoption as sons, by whom we cry, "Abba! Father!" The Spirit himself bears witness with our spirit that we are children of God, and if children, then heirs—heirs of God and fellow heirs with Christ, provided we suffer with him in order that we may also be glorified with him. *(Romans 8:15-17)*

Then shall your light break forth like the dawn, and your healing shall spring up speedily; your righteousness shall go before you; the glory of the LORD shall be your rear guard. Then you shall call, and the LORD will answer; you shall cry, and he will say, "Here I am." …if you pour yourself out for the hungry and satisfy the desire of the afflicted, then shall your light rise in the darkness and your gloom be as the noonday. And the LORD will guide you continually and satisfy your desire in scorched places and make your bones strong; and you shall be like a watered garden, like a spring of water, whose waters do not fail. *(Isaiah 58:8-9a, 10-11)*

See also—Psalm 139:13, Isaiah 49:15-16, Psalm 68:5-6a, II Corinthians 1:3-4

Formed for a Family

(for Sue Callender, based on her favorite scriptures)

"My child, you're still My child, although you now are grown,
And I'm the perfect Parent—unlike the two you've known.
When you were young, they left you often on your own,
But as My child, you never were truly left alone.

"I knitted you together in your mother's womb;
'Twas I who took you out when you needed elbowroom.
A mother's love may not this fallen world withstand,
But I've engraved you on the very palm of My hand.

"I am the Father to the lonely child with none;
I give a home and family to those who don't have one.
When mom and dad forsake, because of death or sin,
Then I, the LORD, will take you right up and take you in.

"For the Spirit you received did not make you a slave,
But you've received the Spirit of adoption that I gave.
With freedom as a son, you won't fall back to fear.
Now you cry, 'Abba! Father!' and I call, 'I am here!'

" 'The Father of Compassion' I am also named;
I comfort you so you'll comfort those whom suffering's maimed.
In entering My family, you've found peace and rest.
Becoming like My Son, you've My heart for the oppressed.

"Now, you're a warrior where the battle lines are drawn;
You kneel to pray then stand to defend the preyed upon.
You've chosen to loose bonds and seek for yokes to break,
So I'll reward your work to free captives for My sake.

"Your healing shall spring forth, and light break over all;
My glory guards your back, and I'll answer when you call.
Your light shall rise in darkness; gloom shall not prevail,
And you'll be like a spring—one whose waters do not fail.

"My Spirit testifies with yours that you are Mine.
You bear the Family likeness—you're letting your light shine.
On earth, My precious child, you've learned I'm always there;
And soon, you'll live in Glory, for you are now My heir!"

37

The eyes of the LORD are toward the righteous and his ears toward their cry.   *(Psalm 34:15)*

I have set the LORD always before me; because he is at my right hand, I shall not be shaken.
(Psalm 16:8)

But God, being rich in mercy, because of the great love with which he loved us, even when we were dead in our trespasses, made us alive together with Christ—by grace you have been saved—   *(Ephesians 2:4-5)*

Be kind to one another, tenderhearted, forgiving one another, as God in Christ forgave you.
(Ephesians 4:32)

Because you are precious in my eyes, and honored, and I love you, I give men in return for you, peoples in exchange for your life.   *(Isaiah 43:4)*

His delight is not in the strength of the horse, nor his pleasure in the legs of a man, but the LORD takes pleasure in those who fear him, in those who hope in his steadfast love.   *(Psalm 147:10-11)*

See also—Ephesians 1:3-6, 5:22-32; Zephaniah 3:17, II Timothy 4:7, Revelation 21:4-5

Drawing Near to the God who is Near to Me

(based on a sermon outline by Dr. Gary Gulbranson)

I often see You as distant—far:
High in heaven, while I am on earth.
Yet, You've tried to show me how near you are
From the moment You called for my birth.
And it's closer still that You want to be,
For You want to have what's called intimacy.

You have called me "Child"—your adopted son,
So, my Lord calls me brother and friend.
Yet, another image you've used is one
That's so close I cannot comprehend:
For all those who now do in Christ abide
Have been made His Body, His Church, and His Bride!

You have shown how intimacy is made:
First, by focus on one whom we love.
Thus, redemption's plan before time was laid—
It was me You were then thinking of.
And You say: on me You have set Your eyes,
While Your ears are open to all of my cries.

My own focus, then, is another sign,
For this closeness requires my part, too.
You have promised that perfect peace is mine
When my mind always stays upon You.
So, in love, You've told me to fix my eyes
Upon You, the One who's my ultimate prize!

Yet, You cannot ever be close to sin,
Thus, I come needing You to forgive.
By Christ's sacrifice, I am clean within;
Your Son died so that I can now live.
With free will, I sinned—needed You to save,
So, Christ paid it all, and You freely forgave.

Now, in me, forgiveness is not toward You;
I forgive those who sin against me.
As Your child, I walk in a path that's new:
To love all as You love is the key.
Christ said I'll forgive other men their sins
When I truly know how You've taken me in.

Feelings, too, must join in this close-knit tie:
You have said I am dear in Your sight.
I'm imperfect, yet You declare that I
Give You joy, and You take great delight.
You've such love for those who do hear Your voice
That You sing o'er them, and in them You rejoice!

Then, as one who loves desires love returned,
So Your greatest command's that I would
Love You now with all of my heart; I've learned
That such love equals my highest good.
I desire to love You with all my strength
Since, for me, Your love went to infinite length!

A relationship of such depth partakes
Of true faithfulness: loyalty's heart.
You are faithful, and every day that breaks
Your new mercies are there at the start.
Since Your steadfast love will not ever cease,
I can rest in You and have unending peace.

I have often failed to keep faith with You,
Yet You're faithful and just to forgive.
I aspire to have, though, a heart that's true,
Keeping faith for as long as I live.
And, since faithfulness is Your Spirit's fruit,
My sure victory's won in this lifelong pursuit.

Then, my spirit's intimacy with You
Will eternally, forever last.
Christ redeemed me, so now death's hold is through;
You'll renew all things—tears will be past.
Now, I'll do Your will, which is Love's design,
For now, I am Yours and, what's more, You are mine!

Therefore, since we have been justified by faith, we have peace with God through our Lord Jesus Christ. *(Romans 5:1)*

Great peace have those who love your law; nothing can make them stumble. *(Psalm 119:165)*

[D]o not be anxious about anything, but in everything by prayer and supplication with thanksgiving let your requests be made known to God. And the peace of God, which surpasses all understanding, will guard your hearts and your minds in Christ Jesus. *(Philippians 4:6-7)*

You keep him in perfect peace whose mind is stayed on you, because he trusts in you. *(Isaiah 26:3)*

"Peace I leave with you; my peace I give to you. Not as the world gives do I give to you. Let not your hearts be troubled, neither let them be afraid." *(John 14:27)*

"I have said these things to you, that in me you may have peace. In the world you will have tribulation. But take heart; I have overcome the world." *(John 16:33)*

See also—Isaiah 48:18, Romans 8:6, Colossians 3:15

The Practice of Peace

I know that the Spirit bears peace as fruit,
Yet I search for peace in a fruitless pursuit.
I pray for serenity; then I find
Many fears and worries still prey on my mind.

What, first, must I know about peace within?
I need peace with God, or I'm lost in my sin.
By faith, I have peace with my God through Christ,
Who has bought that peace with His blood sacrificed.

I'm now a true child of the God of peace,
But does inner turmoil just instantly cease?
My Father defers to my freedom still:
To abide in peace now requires my will.

I search in God's Word for the peace He gives,
And I find that peace does involve how I live.
God wants for me peace that securely stands,
So He gives conditions for peace and commands.

If I will obey all the laws God chose,
I'll have peace sustained like a river that flows.
God promised His statutes would liberate;
When I love God's law, then my peace will be great.

"Be anxious for nothing," I'm told. Instead,
Bring requests to Him who provides daily bread.
God's peace that's beyond what I comprehend
Will then guard my heart and my mind without end.

With mind stayed on God, trusting Him alone,
I'll be kept in peace by my God as His own.
My mind on the Spirit's what peace requires,
For it's death to focus on earthly desires.

The Prince of Peace vowed, "I give peace to you."
But, "Let not your hearts be disturbed," He said, too.
Unlike the world's peace was this gift He made.
With it came the charge, "And do not be afraid."

In Christ is true peace; when affliction's hurled,
It remains, for He's overcome this whole world.
And so, as God's child who is called apart,
I will let Christ's peace rule and reign in my heart!

He rescued me from my strong enemy, from those who hated me, for they were too mighty for me. They confronted me in the day of my calamity, but the LORD was my support. He brought me out into a broad place; he rescued me, because he delighted in me. *(II Samuel 22:18-20)*

Have I not commanded you? Be strong and courageous. Do not be frightened, and do not be dismayed, for the LORD your God is with you wherever you go. *(Joshua 1:9)*

The LORD is my light and my salvation; whom shall I fear? The LORD is the stronghold of my life; of whom shall I be afraid? *(Psalm 27:1)*

I will instruct you and teach you in the way you should go; I will counsel you with my eye upon you. *(Psalm 32:8)*

The grass withers, the flower fades, but the word of our God will stand forever. *(Isaiah 40:8)*

See also—Genesis 15:1, Deuteronomy 7:9, II Chronicles 20:17, Micah 6:8, Joel 2:25, Psalm 127:1

Restored through Relationship

(for Susan Brunsman, based on her favorite scriptures)

"As a child, in your pain you cried out to Me,
And I answered, 'My daughter, don't fear.
Know that I am your shield and your great reward.'
You said, 'Speak, for your servant will hear.'"

"Lord, I called out to You for You'd first called me;
You're my Shepherd, and I knew Your voice.
And I knew of Your strength and Your steadfast love—
You're my God, and I made You my choice.

"With no earthly protection, no human help,
All alone, I had doubted my worth.
Then I found that my help comes from You, the LORD—
From the One who made heaven and earth."

"As you grew, you did learn I'm the faithful God;
In My love, I keep covenant with you
And with all those who love Me and keep My laws—
I commit to your offspring thus, too."

"Lord, you came to my aid, and you rescued me
From my enemies' hate and great might.
You supported me, Father; you brought me out—
You did save, for in me You delight."

"Since you trust in My help, I command, 'Be strong
And take courage; do not be afraid.
I am with you, My child, every place you go;
You've My presence, do not be dismayed.'"

"Yes, O Lord, You're my light—my salvation, too.
Shall I fear any thing that's been made?
You are also the stronghold, the strength of my life,
So, of whom shall I now be afraid?"

"Your whole life is a battle you need not fight.
Child, stand firm, hold your place, and you'll see
The salvation I'll fashion on your behalf.
You will face life with Me: that's the key."

"You have told me, O Lord, what is good to You;
Your requirement's what I want to do:
With Your help, I'll love mercy and do what's just,
And then humbly I'll walk close to You."

"Child, I love your pure heart as you worship Me.
You live truly and do not deceive.
You enjoy a right standing with Me, your God,
And My blessing you now do receive.

"I'll instruct you and teach you the way to go;
I'll give counsel in all that you start.
You've delighted yourself in your loving Lord,
So I'll give the desires of your heart.

"I'll restore all the years that the locust ate
When your life seemed to crumble like sand.
Trust this promise for, though all on earth will fade,
It's My Word that forever will stand."

"Lord, I know that unless You do build my house,
All my labor will just be in vain.
Since my house will be built on Your Word's firm rock
It will stand through all storms, floods, and strain."

"Child, your whole lifetime through, you'd invite Me in,
And you've done what I've told you to do;
So, I'll use all the trials that I've allowed
To do miracles—making you new."

"God, I waited with patience for you to come;
You leaned down, and You heard every cry.
Then, You drew me right out of that miry pit—
Set my feet on a rock up on high."

"Yes, I've heard every prayer, and I hear you now
Ask that others may be thus restored.
They will hear the new song of My praise you sing
And, through you, put their trust in your Lord!"

Jesus said to them, "My food is to do the will of him who sent me and to accomplish his work."
(John 4:34)

"My sheep hear my voice, and I know them, and they follow me. I give them eternal life, and they will never perish, and no one will snatch them out of my hand. My Father, who has given them to me, is greater than all, and no one is able to snatch them out of the Father's hand. I and the Father are one."
(John 10:27-30)

There is neither Jew nor Greek, there is neither slave nor free, there is no male and female, for you are all one in Christ Jesus.
(Galatians 3:28)

"Let not your hearts be troubled. Believe in God; believe also in me. In my Father's house are many rooms. If it were not so, would I have told you that I go to prepare a place for you? And if I go and prepare a place for you, I will come again and will take you to myself, that where I am you may be also."
(John 14:1-3)

See also—John 15:11, Romans 12:4-5, John 20:29

Hearing the High Priestly Prayer

(adapted from John 17:1-24)

When Jesus had finished His final class
With "In Me you have peace" as its sum,
He lifted His eyes up to heaven's throne,
Saying, "Father, the hour has come.

"So, glorify Me that the Son may, too,
Bring You glory just as We had planned;
You gave Me authority over men
To give life to those placed in My hand.

"The life that's eternal is knowing You—
The true God—and the Christ You have sent.
I glorified You on the earth and did
All Your work; for You called, and I went.

"Now glorify Me, Father, with Yourself
With the glory I had then with You
Before earth existed and time began—
Ere man fell and I came to pursue.

"Your Name I've revealed to the ones You gave—
Yours they were, and You gave them to Me.
These precious ones truly have kept Your word.
All I have is from You: this they see.

"I've given to them all the words You gave;
What You gave unto Me they've received.
They know now in truth that I came from You:
That You sent Me they've truly believed.

"It's not for the world that I pray, but them,
For I'm not in the world anymore—
But they will remain in the world, while I
Am now coming to You as before.

"Keep them in Your name, which You've given Me,
So that they'll become one, as We're one.
I've kept them and guarded them—none was lost,
But the one called destruction's true son.

"But now, I am coming back up to You,
So, while still in the world, thus I speak
That they'll find My joy is fulfilled in them—
Joy that comes when it's You that they seek.

"They're not of the world, just as I am not.
I'm not asking that You would just take
Them out of the world; rather, keep them safe
From the evil one's schemes, for My sake.

"Thus, sanctify them through the truth; indeed,
It's Your word that is truth for each heart.
For their sake, I consecrate Myself,
That through truth they may be set apart.

"I make My request, not for these alone,
But for those who'll believe through their word,
So they may be one and may be in Us—
I mean those who've not seen but have heard.

"I've given the glory You gave Me to them;
For their unity, it is the key.
By this, the world knows: I've been sent by You,
And you loved them as You have loved Me.

"O, Father, the ones You have given Me—
I desire them to be where I am,
To see My great glory that's from Your love
Of Your Son who's their Passover Lamb."

When Jesus had spoken these words, He went
To the garden—an obedient Son.
Each boon He had asked was granted, for there:
Not His will, but His Father's was done!

For we do not want you to be ignorant, brothers, of the affliction we experienced in Asia. For we were so utterly burdened beyond our strength that we despaired of life itself. Indeed, we felt that we had received the sentence of death. But that was to make us rely not on ourselves but on God raises the dead.   *(II Corinthians 1:8-9)*

But [the Lord] said to me, "My grace is sufficient for you, for my power is made perfect in weakness." Therefore I will boast all the more gladly of my weaknesses, so that the power of Christ may rest upon me. For the sake of Christ, then, I am content with weaknesses, insults, hardships, persecutions, and calamities. For when I am weak, then I am strong.
                                                                         (II Corinthians 12:9-10)

And we know that for those who love God all things work together for good, for those who are called according to his purpose. For those whom he foreknew he also predestined to be conformed to the image of his Son, in order that he might be the firstborn among many brothers.
                                                                         (Romans 8:28-29)

So we do not lose heart. Though our outer self is wasting away, our inner self is being renewed day by day. For this light momentary affliction is preparing for us an eternal weight of glory beyond all comparison…   *(II Corinthians 4:16-17)*

See also—Psalm 62:8, Psalm 55:17, II Corinthians 4:7, 10; Philippians 2:5-8, Job 23:10

The Groaning, the Good, and the Glory

(dedicated to John and Sondra Beck, as they were fighting John's battle with cancer)

It's the question it seems I should never ask,
For to do so would seem to take God to task.
Yet I can't stop myself; I blurt, "But, God, why?"
And it comes as a shout, a whisper, or cry:

"Why must my problem be inside, not out?
Why must it challenge my faith—make me doubt?
Why must I be and feel broken, not whole?
Why so defective in mind and in soul?

"Why am I able to do so much good,
Yet, I so oft can't do what I once could?
Doesn't God want me to give and to serve?
Isn't that what friends and family deserve?"

Then, I think of my peers and how I compare,
Though I've seen that this path just feeds my despair.
I begin to believe God sees, but won't care,
For it seems that He doesn't answer my prayer.

Yet the psalmist did say, "Pour out your full heart
Before God who's our refuge—God won't depart!"
So, at night, morn and noon, he made it his choice
To complain to his God, for God hears each voice!

Now, my God also makes His voice clearly heard
As He personalizes His Holy Word.
I don't always remember all He has said,
But God's given me answers as I have read:

Paul was burdened, distressed; despaired with
    each breath,
For he felt he'd received the sentence of death.
Then, Paul found 'twas to make him trust—so he said—
Not in man, but in God, who raises the dead!

Then, God's grace did suffice Paul's suffering to meet
For, in weakness, God's pow'r is made all complete.
When I'm weak, then Christ's power rests upon me;
Thus, when weak, I am strong: Christ's strength all
    will see.

God declares, "For your good, all things I'll align,
For you love Me; I've called you by My design."
But just what's His good plan for all of life's storms?
That my life to Christ's image fully conforms.

We are told we've God's light in jars made of clay,
So, "The power is God's, not theirs," all will say.
And we bear in our frames Christ's death ever fresh,
That Christ's life may be shown to all in our flesh.

Paul claimed, "I won't lose heart; my flesh does decay,
But my inner, true self's renewed day by day.
For this light, brief affliction now does prepare
The incomparable glory I'll ever share."

In Christ's model, I've seen that God's perfect plan
Did require Christ be weak, for He became man!
Then His flesh couldn't do what He before could,
But these limits accomplished ultimate good!

If, then, Paul and my Lord did suffer, were weak,
I should not for a trial-free life always seek.
For, "My God knows my path," by Job I am told,
"And so when He has tried me, I'll come forth
    as gold!"

Blessed be the God and Father of our Lord Jesus Christ, who has blessed us in Christ with every spiritual blessing in the heavenly places, even as he chose us in him before the foundation of the world, that we should be holy and blameless before him.   *(Ephesians 1:3-4)*

For the Son of God, Jesus Christ, whom we proclaimed among you, Silvanus and Timothy and I, was not Yes and No, but in him it is always Yes. For all the promises of God find their Yes in him. That is why it is through him that we utter our Amen to God for his glory.
(II Corinthians 1:19-20)

Now may the God of peace who brought again from the dead our Lord Jesus, the great shepherd of the sheep, by the blood of the eternal covenant, equip you with everything good that you may do his will, working in us that which is pleasing in his sight, through Jesus Christ, to whom be glory forever and ever. Amen.   *(Hebrews 13:20-21)*

May you be strengthened with all power, according to [God's] glorious might, for all endurance and patience with joy, giving thanks to the Father, who has qualified you to share in the inheritance of the saints in light.   *(Colossians 1:11-12)*

Now may the Lord of peace himself give you peace at all times in every way. The Lord be with you all.   *(II Thessalonians 3:16)*

Benedictions to Believe

Benedictions and blessings are nice ways to end,
But which blessings are ones on which you can depend?
Just the blessings God wrote in His Word we find true;
They accord with God's will, so they're what He will do.

Since our peace with God is through Christ now restored,
Every spiritual blessing is ours in our Lord.
These inspired benedictions give God's vows to bless,
For, in Christ, every promise does find its true "Yes!"

May the God of hope now entirely fill
You with all joy and peace as you trust in Him still,
So that by the great power the Holy Ghost shows
You abound in all hope, and it then overflows.

May our Lord Himself and our God, who did give
Us great comfort, good hope, and the grace now to live,
Therefore comfort your hearts and establish them, too,
Now in every good word and good work that you'll do.

May the God of peace who raised Christ from the dead,
By the blood of the covenant which He did shed,
Now equip you with everything good that you may
Then perform His true will through our Lord every day.

May the God of peace wholly sanctify you—
Your whole spirit, soul, body keep blamelessly, too
When Christ comes. He who calls you is faithful and true;
Therefore, all He has promised He surely will do!

But Jesus looked at [the disciples] and said, "With man this is impossible, but with God all things are possible." *(Matthew 19:26)*

For this reason I remind you to fan into flame the gift of God, which is in you through the laying on of my hands, for God gave us a spirit not of fear but of power and love and self-control. *(II Timothy 1:6-7)*

For the eyes of the LORD run to and fro throughout the whole earth, to give strong support to those whose heart is blameless toward him. *(II Chronicles 16:9a)*

Let us then with confidence draw near to the throne of grace, that we may receive mercy and find grace to help in time of need. *(Hebrews 4:16)*

Thus says the LORD: "Let not the wise man boast in his wisdom, let not the mighty man boast in his might, let not the rich man boast in his riches, but let him who boasts boast in this, that he understands and knows me, that I am the LORD who practices steadfast love, justice, and righteousness in the earth. For in these things I delight, declares the LORD." *(Jeremiah 9:23-24)*

See also—Ephesians 3:17-19, Psalm 139:17-18, Philippians 1:6, Isaiah 6:8

Song for a Surrendered Servant

(for a pastor's wife, based on her favorite scriptures)

"Come to Me, My child; I'm He who saves.
Watch My joy in you pour out in waves.
Now rest in My love where you belong,
And hear Me rejoice over you in song.

"When I formed you, I made a wanted child;
Yet you're fallen, so come—be reconciled.
Fear not, your redemption's My design.
I've called you by name, and you are Mine.

"You're so precious that I won't let go;
Hence I paid a price your mind can't know.
It bought more than you can understand:
Your name is engraved upon My hand.

"And I saved you for a holy call,
Not according to your works at all:
Instead, by My purpose and the grace
I gave you in Christ before time and space.

"But My path for you has many tasks;
You may fear you'll break from all it asks.
Impossible, yes, it is—with man;
With Me, you can do all things I plan.

"For I did not give the spirit of fear:
It can find no place when I am here.
My power and love you have inside;
Since fear's taken flight, sound mind presides.

"So with all your heart, put trust in Me;
Don't rely on what you think and see.
Acknowledge Me, then, in all your ways—
Your paths I'll direct for all your days.

"For, throughout the earth, My eyes will run,
Seeking those who say, 'Thy will be done.'
I strongly support the ones whose heart
Is blameless toward Me and won't depart.

"Thus, I see how boldly you draw near
To My throne of grace, and I will hear.
You ask and receive, for trust succeeds
At finding the grace to meet your needs.

"Then, secured in love, you'll comprehend
What's the length and breadth of love I send
To you in My Son, so you'll be filled
With fullness from Him whose blood was spilled.

"You'll be filled each day with all you need,
So your life can be quite free of greed—
Content with such things as you receive,
For I don't forsake and never leave.

"So then, seek the pure and lovely ways,
Things of good report—those worth My praise,
The ones that with truth and honor ring:
I made you to think on all such things.

"Yes, I'm pleased My thoughts are dear to you;
You could count each day your whole life through,
But finding their sum exceeds your skill.
Relax and you'll see you're with Me still.

"And since I'm with you, don't be afraid;
I am still your God—be not dismayed.
I'll give you My strength and help you stand
And always uphold with My right hand.

"Though you're strong and wise, you must not miss
That the one who boasts must boast in this:
You know Me as LORD—*I reign above;*
I'm righteous and act with steadfast love.

"As you run your race, you can be sure:
I began this work—it will endure.
I promise that you will be complete
That day when My Son, your Lord, you meet.

"Now, you've served each day, and month, and year
With the joyful call, 'Send me—I'm here!'
With grace, you've performed as pastor's wife;
Far more, you have led a Christ-like life!"

Remember these things, O Jacob, and Israel, for you are my servant; I formed you; you are my servant; O Israel, you will not be forgotten by me. I have blotted out your transgressions like a cloud and your sins like mist; return to me, for I have redeemed you.   *(Isaiah 44:21-22)*

Blessed is the nation whose God is the LORD, the people whom he has chosen as his heritage!   *(Psalm 33:12)*

Blessed is he whose help is the God of Jacob, whose hope is in the LORD his God, who made heaven and earth, the sea, and all that is in them, who keeps faith forever; who executes justice for the oppressed, who gives food to the hungry.   *(Psalm 146:5-7a)*

For the LORD takes pleasure in his people; he adorns the humble with salvation.   *(Psalm 149:4)*

"But seek first the kingdom of God and his righteousness, and all these things will be added to you."   *(Matthew 6:33)*

The Prophet of Priorities

(based on the book of Haggai)

God's people had returned—restored to their land;
The word of the LORD next came by Haggai's hand:
"Thus says the LORD of hosts: These people do grouse,
'The time's not yet come to rebuild the LORD's house.'"

"Is this a time," God asked, "for you here to dwell
At ease while, behold—My house lies where it fell?
Consider then your ways: you choose your own will,
Then sow, eat and drink, but never have your fill.

"Thus says the LORD of hosts: Consider your ways.
Go, bring wood and build the house that brings Me praise.
I have proclaimed a drought on all that you've grown:
My house lies decayed, but you just build your own."

The people and their head obeyed their God's voice,
And, fearing the LORD, they made His plan their choice.
Then, Haggai spoke again—new hope to record;
This next message read, "I'm with you, says the LORD."

Again the LORD's word came: "Are you now distraught?
Compared to the first, this temple seems as naught?
Yet now, all you be strong—work, for I'm with you.
My covenant stands, so trust My promise true.

"The glory of this house will come to outshine
The rich one that was, for all that's wealth is Mine.
Declares the LORD of hosts: With glory's increase,
As well, in this place, to you I will give peace.

"Consider from now on: How did you then fare
Before stones were placed to build My temple there?
Your harvest yield was half of what you'd foresee;
Though blight and hail came, you did not turn to Me.

"Consider from now on: since first you laid stone
To build Me My house, what harvest is your own?
Your crops have yielded naught, no wine in the press;
But now you've obeyed—from this day on I'll bless!"

To Samuel, God had said, "I look on the heart."
So God's plan has been a people set apart,
With their priority: His work, not their own—
For they're only His when God is on their throne.

We worry that our needs may suffer neglect,
Yet putting self first won't yield what we expect.
Since God most wants us close, as prophets have told:
To turn us to Him, His blessings He'll withhold.

And so, declared God's Son, "Obey what I say:
Seek God's kingdom first—that is the only way.
With righteousness your goal, you'll come and find rest;
I'll meet all your needs, and you'll be truly blessed!"

No man shall be able to stand before you all the days of your life. Just as I was with Moses, so I will be with you. I will not leave you or forsake you. *(Joshua 1:5)*

But the LORD said to [Jeremiah], "Do not say, 'I am only a youth'; for to all to whom I send you, you shall go, and whatever I command you, you shall speak. Do not be afraid of them, for I am with you to deliver you, declares the LORD." *(Jeremiah 1:7-8)*

All this took place to fulfill what the Lord had spoken by the prophet: "Behold, the virgin shall conceive and bear a son, and they shall call his name Immanuel" (which means, God with us). *(Matthew 1:22-23)*

And Jesus came and said to [the eleven disciples], "All authority in heaven and on earth has been given to me. Go therefore and make disciples of all nations, baptizing them in the name of the Father and of the Son and of the Holy Spirit, teaching them to observe all that I have commanded you. And behold, I am with you always, to the end of the age." *(Matthew 28:18-20)*

See also—Genesis 26:24, 28:13-15; Exodus 3:10-12, 4:15; Isaiah 41:10, Haggai 2:4,6-9, Acts 18:9-10

A Chronicle of Closeness

Our questions keep endlessly circling, it seems:
"Will I ever fulfill all my hopes and my dreams?
I don't know the way—how am I supposed to lead?
Where's the money and wisdom and strength that I need?"

"God's Word has the answers," we're told. But just where?
We find so many stories and statutes in there!
Yet, over and over, this vow we have read:
To each person in need, "I am with you," God said.

While Isaac was moving, God came to express,
"Do not fear, for I'm with you to guide and to bless.
As God of your father, this promise I make:
I will multiply offspring to you for his sake."

In Jacob's famed dream, God said, "I am the LORD.
I will give you this region which you have explored.
Behold, I am with you to guard on your way,
And I won't ever leave till I've done what I say."

The LORD called to Moses, "I've heard Israel's cry;
You will go." But then Moses complained, "Who am I?"
God spoke, not about what all Moses could do;
He said, "I'll be your teacher, and I'll be with you."

To Joshua, God pledged, "Not one person can stand
Now against you as you go to conquer this land.
I'll never forsake you—you'll lead Israel through.
Just as I was with Moses, so I'll be with you."

Next, Gideon heard, "The LORD's with you, brave man."
He responded, "But I am the least in my clan."
God answered, "But I will be with you indeed,
So, to vanquish your foes, you have all that you need."

When Babylon threatened, God said, "Do not fear.
Israel, I am your God, and I'm with you—I'm here.
I'll strengthen you, help you, and I will uphold
With My hand, which is righteous, so you can be bold."

God called Jeremiah, who claimed, "I'm a youth."
God replied, "You will go, and you'll speak all My truth.
Do not be afraid of them—I'm with you now.
I'll deliver, for you have been chosen, I vow."

"Fear not," said the LORD. "Israel, be not dismayed.
You'll be saved from the land where your captives
        had stayed.
In quiet and ease, unafraid, you'll return,
For I'm with you to save you, My people shall learn."

The exiles returned, and the LORD spoke: "Be strong.
You must work, for I'm with you. It will not be long:
This new temple's glory soon I will increase,
And I'll fill it with silver and gold, and with peace."

Then, just as to prophets, God's word came to Paul:
"Go on speaking, for you are fulfilling My call.
Do not be afraid, for I'm with you to keep,
So you'll never be harmed as you wake or you sleep."

Long past to the present, the answer's the same;
God is with us—His Son even carries that name:
The Word became flesh, sent among us to dwell,
So the virgin-born Son is called Immanuel.

He died for our sins and then rose from the dead.
"All authority's given to Me," so He said.
"Now teach My disciples till history's last page,
And behold, I am with you to the end of the age!"

I love the LORD, because he has heard my voice and my pleas for mercy. Because he inclined his ear to me, therefore I will call on him as long as I live. The snares of death encompassed me; the pangs of Sheol laid hold on me; I suffered distress and anguish. Then I called on the name of the LORD: "O LORD, I pray, deliver my soul!"   *(Psalm 116:1-4)*

Return, O my soul, to your rest; for the LORD has dealt bountifully with you. For you have delivered my soul from death, my eyes from tears, my feet from stumbling; I will walk before the LORD in the land of the living.   *(Psalm 116:7-9)*

But now, O LORD, you are our Father; we are the clay, and you are our potter; we are all the work of your hand.   *(Isaiah 64:8)*

No temptation has overtaken you that is not common to man. God is faithful, and he will not let you be tempted beyond your ability, but with the temptation he will also provide the way of escape, that you may be able to endure it.   *(I Corinthians 10:13)*

Song of Deliverance

I will love the Lord God, for my voice He has heard.
I was pleading for help, and He kept His Word.
I'll continue to call, for my God bends His ear,
And His answer's enough, for God says, "I'm here."

Chorus:
So, return, O my soul, to your rest;
God's provisions have conquered each test.
When God calls, and my answer is "Yes,"
I will find all He wills is to bless.

I was bound by my pain, nearly trapped in death's snare.
I began to believe that my God's not there.
In despair, yet I called on the name of the Lord—
He who raises the dead simply snapped death's cord.

Thus, my God has delivered my soul out of death.
He provides what I need as I draw each breath.
Though my eyes swim with tears, I will not ever drown,
For His grace lifts me up every time I'm down.

Though the path where He leads may seem dark, it is best;
I'm God's child and His clay, molded by life's tests.
Through each trial and hardship God has made a way,
And He's used them to shape who I am today.

Looking back at my life, I can see all God gave—
Whether blessing or pain—was His way to save.
Though I suffer, I'm safe in God's merciful care,
For He'll never allow more than I can bear!

For there is no distinction: for all have sinned and fall short of the glory of God, and are justified by his grace as a gift, through the redemption that is in Christ Jesus, whom God put forward as a propitiation by his blood, to be received by faith. *(Romans 3:22b-25a)*

But we ought always to give thanks to God for you, brothers beloved by the Lord, because God chose you as the firstfruits to be saved, through sanctification by the Spirit and belief in the truth. To this he called you through our gospel, so that you may obtain the glory of our Lord Jesus Christ. *(II Thessalonians 2:13-14)*

There is therefore now no condemnation for those who are in Christ Jesus. For the law of the Spirit of life has set you free in Christ Jesus from the law of sin and death. *(Romans 8:1-2)*

The former priests were many in number, because they were prevented by death from continuing in office, but [Jesus] holds his priesthood permanently, because he continues forever. Consequently, he is able to save to the uttermost those who draw near to God through him, since he always lives to make intercession for them. *(Hebrews 7:23-25)*

In this the love of God was made manifest among us, that God sent his only Son into the world, so that we might live through him. In this is love, not that we have loved God but that he loved us and sent his Son to be the propitiation for our sins. *(I John 4:9-10)*

Saved and Secure

(adapted from Romans 8:28-39)

We know that for those who do love their great Lord
Surely all works together for good,
For those whose true call with His purpose accords.
The Lord does all He said that He would.

For those He foreknew He predestined, then, too
To be truly conformed to His Son,
So He'd be the firstborn of many, not few.
This: the good that God meant for each one.

And those He predestined He also did call,
Those He called He did justify, too;
Those justified—He also glorified all.
God completes what He started to do.

To all of these truths, then, just what shall we say?
If God's for us, who can be our foe?
He spared not His Son—gave Him up that dark day,
So He'll give us all things, this we know.

Thus, who brings a charge now against God's elect?
God has justified—we're condemned how?
Christ died and was raised, so there's none to reject;
Christ indeed intercedes for us now.

Who separates us from the love of our Lord?
Shall great trials, afflictions, distress,
Or famine or nakedness, danger, or sword?
"We're regarded as those to oppress."

No, in all of these things we are conquerors and more
Through the One who has loved us: I'm sure
Not death, nor this life, nor the angels that soar,
Nor things now, nor things yet to endure,

Nor depths of the sea, nor the heights up above—
Nothing else that creation has stored,
Is able to separate us from God's love,
Which is ours in Christ Jesus our Lord!

59

"Come to me, all who labor and are heavy laden, and I will give you rest. Take my yoke upon you, and learn from me, for I am gentle and lowly in heart, and you will find rest for your souls. For my yoke is easy, and my burden is light." *(Matthew 11:28-30)*

Listen to me, O house of Jacob, all the remnant of the house of Israel, who have been borne by me from before your birth, carried from the womb; even to your old age I am he, and to gray hairs I will carry you. I have made, and I will bear; I will carry and will save. *(Isaiah 46:3-4)*

I love you, O LORD, my strength. The LORD is my rock and my fortress and my deliverer, my God, my rock, in whom I take refuge, my shield, and the horn of my salvation, my stronghold. *(Psalm 18:1-2)*

When the righteous cry for help, the LORD hears and delivers them out of all their troubles. *(Psalm 34:17)*

You who have made me see many troubles and calamities will revive me again; from the depths of the earth you will bring me up again. You will increase my greatness and comfort me again. *(Psalm 71:20-21)*

See also—II Corinthians 1:19-20, Romans 15:5-6, Isaiah 49:16, Psalm 118:17-18, Psalm 40:2

A Very Present Hope

(for a friend)

What do you do when you can't bear the pain?
How can you break your perpetual chain?
Where do you go when there's nowhere to turn?
How can you live through the nth "crash and burn"?

There is no easy answer——no pat cliché
That can bind up the wounds from this world's dark decay.
No, your answers can't come from the earth at all;
They are found in the God who will answer each call.

He's the God whose own Son came to bear all pain
And wash clean with His blood every blot of sin's stain.
Now God's power to heal can come in——restore,
For between you and God's not a wall but the Door!

You may feel overwhelmed by your suffering's sum,
But Christ vowed that He had this dark world overcome.
There's still pain, yet, in Christ, you'll have all you need,
For in Christ is the "Yes!" for each promise we read.

Are you bound by the anguish of heart or flesh?
He's the "God of all comfort" with balm ever fresh.
Gripped by fear, worried sick, and then in despair?
"God of peace," "God of hope"——He will meet you
     right there.

Been enslaved by the pow'r of habitual sin?
God has given His Spirit to change you within.
Just one link at a time your chain breaks——each length?
He's the God of endurance, encouragement, strength!

Finding no one to help; problems all you see?
Heavy laden and worn? Christ calls out, "Come to Me!"
You'll find rest for your soul and His wisdom, too.
You will bear His light yoke, but then He'll carry you!

God's your rock and your fortress, your light, your shield——
He just asks that you trust Him and thus learn to yield.
You can know when you call you'll be heard and saved
By the One on whose palms your own name is engraved.

Are your life and your soul in such awful shape
That you're tempted to take now the final escape?
Though you feel the Lord's discipline with each breath,
The Lord hasn't and won't give you over to death!

When you feel that you've reached your last inch of rope,
Not in self nor in things, but in God place your hope.
He will save you again from this pit of strife;
God has saved you from death——now He'll save you
     through life!

Saved to Surrender, Strengthened to Serve

(for Lynn Lane, based on her favorite scriptures)

"Child, you came to Me when you were grown,
Yet you know you are no less My own.
You now have My Son and trust His name,
So, you know My life's replaced your shame.

"Jesus is My Son—this truth you tell,
So, My home's in you; in Me, you dwell.
You're His sheep and hear His voice each day;
You are known by Him, and you obey."

"Lord, I'm crucified with Christ—set free!
It's not I who live, but Christ in me.
Now, the way I live is to rely
On Your Son whose love brought Him to die.

"And now, let the words that my mouth speaks
And my heart's each thought and what it seeks
Be acceptable within Your sight,
My redeemer, LORD, my rock, my light."

"You do please Me, child, with what you do,
For you love each one as Christ's loved you.
Thus, you honor what He did command,
So, He calls you 'friend;' you're in His hand.

"And you are like Christ: without conceit,
As you humbly serve all those you meet.
I regard the low, although I'm high—
From the proud, I'm far; to you, I'm nigh."

"LORD, I'll give You thanks with my whole heart,
For Your steadfast love will not depart.
I have trusted in that love You gave,
And my heart rejoices as You save."

"Yes, it's all your trust that I demand;
You can't lean on what you understand.
So, acknowledge Me in all your ways;
I'll direct your paths for all your days.

"My commands will help you make each choice:
First, rejoice in Me; I say, rejoice!
Then, be anxious for nothing—you must rest,
And in prayer with thanks, bring Me requests.

"Thus, My peace surpassing thought you'll find,
Which, in Christ, will guard your heart and mind.
And whatever's true, or just, or pure,
When you think on these, you will mature."

"Lord, it's safe to do just what You've said—
You're my shield, my glory; You lift my head.
When I cry aloud, You always hear;
Though Your home's on high, Your answer's near.

"God, my strength and refuge, I can know
You will help in every trial and woe.
So, I will not fear, though earth should quake,
The sea's waters roar, or mountains shake."

"Yes, fear not, you're redeemed by My design;
I have called you by name, and you are Mine.
I will be with you through floods you face;
Fire and flame shall not defeat My grace.

"You have walked amid great troubles, strife;
I revived you and preserved your life.
I'll stretch out My hand against your foes;
My right hand will save each one I chose.

"Child, when funds were drained by sad events,
You stayed free of greed and were content,
For you trust that I don't make mistakes,
And I'll never leave you nor forsake!"

"Yes, like Paul, I've learned to be content;
I can do all things with strength Christ's sent.
When I call, Your answer gives me peace,
And my strength of soul You do increase.

"As before, in these new fields I see,
You'll fulfill Your purpose planned for me.
Then, I'll sing to You, my LORD and King—
You've been good to me through everything."

"Child, you've served and prayed; I've seen and heard,
And I've taught you more My will and Word.
I'm so pleased with how you've walked and grown,
And good fruit's been borne by seeds you've sown.

"Now, I'm pleased to use your gifts anew,
And with all My pow'r I'll strengthen you.
You've learned patience from all you've endured;
As you model Christ, your joy's assured."

"I'm your God; I'll meet your needs—each one
With My wealth in glory by My Son.
Daughter, share My light each place I send,
Then, share in My joy that will not end."

"Father, I give thanks as your blest heir.
As a saint, I've now Your light to share.
Lord, deliver men from sin and death
As You use my life—each hour, each breath."

But you, O LORD, are a shield about me, my glory, and the lifter of my head.   *(Psalm 3:3)*

Though I walk in the midst of trouble, you preserve my life; you stretch out your hand against the wrath of my enemies, and your right hand delivers me.   *(Psalm 138:7)*

Not that I am speaking of being in need, for I have learned in whatever situation I am to be content. I know how to be brought low, and I know how to abound. In any and every circumstance, I have learned the secret of facing plenty and hunger, abundance and need. I can do all things through him who strengthens me.   *(Philippians 4:11-13)*

See also—John 10:27-28, Psalm 19:14, Philippians 4:4,6-8; Psalm 46:1-3, Hebrews 13:5

So Jesus said to the Jews who had believed in him, "If you abide in my word, you are truly my disciples, and you will know the truth, and the truth will set you free." *(John 8:31-32)*

And it is my prayer that your love may abound more and more, with knowledge and all discernment, so that you may approve what is excellent, and so be pure and blameless for the day of Christ, filled with the fruit of righteousness that comes through Jesus Christ, to the glory and praise of God. *(Philippians 1:9-11)*

"You did not choose me, but I chose you and appointed you that you should go and bear fruit and that your fruit should abide, so that whatever you ask the Father in my name, he may give it to you." *(John 15:16)*

But the fruit of the Spirit is love, joy, peace, patience, kindness, goodness, faithfulness, gentleness, self-control; against such things there is no law. *(Galatians 5:22-23)*

A Vision of the Vine

(adapted from John 15:1-11)

The night before He was to die,
Christ taught of the life His blood would buy.
He said to His devoted band,
"I am the true vine, so understand:

"My Father is He who tends the vine
So there will be fruit of His design.
Each barren branch in Me He'll excise;
He prunes those which bear so output will rise.

"Already, you've been pruned, made clean,
Because of My word you've heard and seen.
Abide in Me, and when you do,
Your life will be lived as 'I in you.'

"No branch bears fruit when all alone;
It must in the vine abide as grown—
No more can you, without this key:
For fruit-bearing life, Abide in Me!

"I am the vine; the branches are you.
Who dwells now in Me, and I in him, too,
Will bear much fruit, for as I've taught
When separate from Me, you can do naught.

"If one does not in Me abide,
He withers like branches cast aside.
They're thrown into the fire and burned—
The ultimate price for Truth that's spurned.

"If you abide in Me, and when
My words do abide in you, just then
You'll ask for what you wish, I say,
And it will be done when you so pray.

"My Father's praised when you bear much fruit,
Thus proving I am your true pursuit.
And I've loved you, as He's loved Me;
Abide in My love—it's pure and free.

"If you will keep what I command,
You'll abide in My love and in My hand;
So I have kept My Father's decrees
And abide in His love—at rest and at ease.

"And thus, I've told you all these things
That now My own joy in you may sing.
I'll give My all for death's defeat,
So joy—Mine and yours—will be complete."

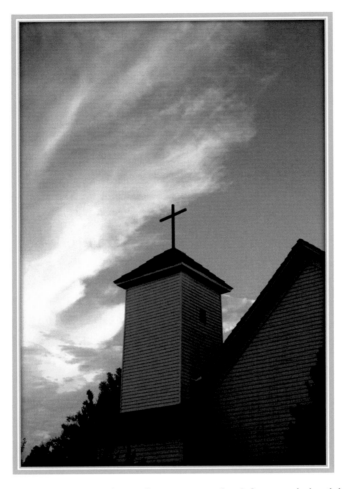

But he was wounded for our transgressions; he was crushed for our iniquities; upon him was the chastisement that brought us peace, and with his stripes we are healed. All we like sheep have gone astray; we have turned—every one—to his own way; and the LORD has laid on him the iniquity of us all…Out of the anguish of his soul he shall see and be satisfied; by his knowledge shall the righteous one, my servant, make many to be accounted righteous, and he shall bear their iniquities. *(Isaiah 53:5-6, 11)*

But in fact Christ has been raised from the dead, the firstfruits of those who have fallen asleep. For as by a man came death, by a man has come also the resurrection of the dead. For as in Adam all die, so also in Christ shall all be made alive. *(I Corinthians 15:20-22)*

We were buried therefore with [Christ] by baptism into death, in order that, just as Christ was raised from the dead by the glory of the Father, we too might walk in newness of life…We know that Christ, being raised from the dead, will never die again; death no longer has dominion over him. *(Romans 6:4, 9)*

But our citizenship is in heaven, and from it we await a Savior, the Lord Jesus Christ, who will transform our lowly body to be like his glorious body, by the power that enables him even to subject all things to himself. *(Philippians 3:20-21)*

Resurrection Reflection

(adapted from John 20:1-31)

"It is finished," He cried as He breathed His last,
And it seemed as if Jesus' whole life was past.
The noon sky had gone black——the temple veil torn
As Christ died: He whose death was why He'd been born.

He'd been laid in a tomb. With the Sabbath gone,
Mary Magdalene came in the early dawn.
When she saw that the stone was taken away,
Mary ran up to John and Peter to say:

"Oh, the Lord has been taken——we don't know where."
So, they ran to the tomb, wondering what was there.
They saw cloths lying there——the cloth for His face
Wasn't with all the rest, but folded in place.

The disciples returned where their homes were kept,
So just Mary stood outside the tomb and wept.
Looking into the tomb, she saw a great sight:
At its head and its foot, two angels in white.

Then they said to her, "Why are your tears outpoured?"
And she answered, "They've taken away my Lord."
Mary then turned around, and Jesus she saw.
She knew not it was He, and looked without awe.

He asked whom she was seeking and why she cried.
"Tell me where you have carried him," she replied.
Jesus spoke to her: "Mary"——simply her name.
Then, just "Master!" she called, as joy overcame.

"Do not cling, for I've yet to ascend," He said.
"But now go to my brothers and say instead:
'I'll ascend to My Father——soon, I will go.'"
She announced, "I have seen the Lord, you must know!"

On that night, Jesus came: "Peace be with you!" He cried.
And He showed His disciples His hands and side.
Once again, "Peace be with you." Then, He said, too:
"As the Father sent Me, so I'm sending you."

But still Thomas proclaimed, "No I won't believe
Till my sight and my touch do His wounds perceive."
Then, to Thomas, Christ showed his wounds just that way,
So, "My Lord and my God!" was all he could say.

Christ replied, "You've believed because now you see?
Blest are those who believe though they don't see Me."
Thus, Christ rose, conquering death. This, the reason
    He came:
That, believing in Him, you'd have life in His name!

Maker and Musician

(for Bev Bothel, when retiring as accompanist of the Westminster Chapel Choir)

"I have searched you and known you, My child;
I'm aware when you sit and you rise.
You can know that My hand's on your life
Even when you cannot see the 'whys.'"

"From my youth, Lord, You've been my true hope;
You've sustained since before my own birth.
When I lift up my eyes and find help,
It's from You, who made heaven and earth."

"Now, be filled with My Spirit and strength;
Let Christ's word in you then richly dwell,
Singing psalms, hymns and songs from your heart,
Giving thanks as My praises you tell."

"It is good to give thanks to You, Lord—
To sing praise to Your name, O Most High.
I'll declare Your great love in the morn
And Your grace when my bedtime is nigh.

"You delight in the music I make.
I will play as You give me the skill.
You've bestowed the desires of my heart;
My delight's in performing Your will."

"I'll fulfill all My purpose for you,
And My love will endure, come what may.
No dark gloom can extinguish My light,
For, with Me, the night's bright as the day."

"Lord, are You in the dark of my womb?
I can't see Your big plan—I'm afraid!
Yet You formed me—I know that You're good;
I am fearfully, wonderfully made."

"Child, his frame is not hidden from Me.
I am knitting your life and your son.
I can see all his hours and days;
They are writ in My book, every one."

"You fulfill Your true purpose for me—
I cry out to You, God, the Most High.
I'll take refuge beneath Your great wings
Till these storms of destruction pass by.

"My soul thirsts for my Lord as for springs.
You uphold me; I'll cling to Your hand.
Yes, my flesh longs for You, O my God,
In a weary and dry desert land."

"Do not fear, I'll give drink to the parched;
I'll pour streams, then, upon the dry ground.
On your offspring, My Spirit I'll pour,
And My blessings to them will compound."

"O my strength, I will sing of Your praise,
And Your love I will sing now aloud,
For Your mercy is great to the heav'ns,
And Your truth reaches up to the clouds."

"Yes, the heavens My glory declare,
And the skies My achievement proclaim,
For I made them with only a word,
And I call every star by its name.

"My own hands formed the sea and the land,
So their heights, depths and wealth are all Mine.
Yet, as sure as I made you, I'll help:
My dear sheep, I'm your shepherd divine."

"Lord, I see You in all that You've made
By Your power and strong, outstretched arm.
I'll be safe in Your Almighty love;
Though I hurt, You will keep me from harm.

"You have given me many new songs,
So among all the nations I'd praise.
I've made many a glad, joyful noise;
I've rejoiced in my God all my days.

"Now, You're calling me to a new role.
I am Yours: I was bought with a price.
I'll obey, for this is how I serve:
As a living, complete sacrifice.

"O my God, from my youth You have led.
I've proclaimed You in word and in deed.
Give me power to show those to come
That their Maker is all that they need!"

"Child, I held you before you were born;
As you age and beyond the dark grave,
I will bear you each step of the way.
I have made; I do carry; I'll save!"

I lift up my eyes to the hills. From where does my help come? My help comes from the LORD, who made heaven and earth. *(Psalm 121:1-2)*

For you formed my inward parts; you knitted me together in my mother's womb. I praise you, for I am fearfully and wonderfully made. Wonderful are your works; my soul knows it very well…Your eyes saw my unformed substance; in your book were written, every one of them, the days that were formed for me, when as yet there was none of them. *(Psalm 139:13-14, 16)*

Be merciful to me, O God, be merciful to me, for in you my soul takes refuge; in the shadow of your wings I will take refuge, till the storms of destruction pass by. I cry out to God Most High, to God who fulfills his purpose for me. *(Psalm 57:1-2)*

Thus says the LORD who made you, who formed you from the womb and will help you: Fear not, O Jacob my servant, Jeshurun whom I have chosen. For I will pour water on the thirsty land, and streams on the dry ground; I will pour my Spirit upon your offspring, and my blessing on your descendants. *(Isaiah 44:2-3)*

See also—Psalm 139:1-6, 59:16-17; Isaiah 40:26, Jeremiah 32:17, Psalm 62:11-12, 71:17-18

For their sake [the LORD] remembered his covenant, and relented according to the abundance of his steadfast love. *(Psalm 106:45)*

"I [the LORD], I am he who blots out your transgressions for my own sake, and I will not remember your sins." *(Isaiah 43:25)*

"Come now, let us reason together, says the LORD: though your sins are like scarlet, they shall be as white as snow; though they are red like crimson, they shall become like wool." *(Isaiah 1:18)*

I will give them a heart to know that I am the LORD, and they shall be my people and I will be their God, for they shall return to me with their whole heart. *(Jeremiah 24:7)*

For thus says the One who is high and lifted up, who inhabits eternity, whose name is Holy: "I dwell in the high and holy place, and also with him who is of a contrite and lowly spirit, to revive the spirit of the lowly, and to revive the heart of the contrite." *(Isaiah 57:15)*

See also—Hebrews 9:13-14, Romans 3:4, I John 1:7, 9

A Record of Repentance
(adapted from Psalm 51:1-14, 16-17)

Have mercy upon me, O God, I pray,
In accord with Your unfailing love.
And as Your great mercy abounds, today
Blot out all that I am guilty of.

Now wash me in full from iniquity
And then cleanse me from sin I despise.
I know my transgressions—they're all I see:
My sin's ever before my own eyes.

I've sinned against You—against only You,
And I've done what's so wrong in Your sight.
Your words, then, are justified; You speak true,
And Your judgment is blameless and right.

To birth I was brought in iniquity,
And my mother conceived me in sin.
You want for the truth to be deep in me,
And You teach me Your wisdom within.

Lord, purify me, and I shall be clean;
When You wash, I'll be whiter than snow.
Let joy now be heard and then gladness seen;
Let the bones that You broke see joy grow.

And then, hide Your face from guilt's path I trod
And blot out from Your sight all my sins.
Create within me a clean heart, O God,
And renew a right spirit within.

Don't cast me away from Your presence, Lord,
And don't take Your Holy Spirit away.
Salvation's pure joy—let it be restored;
Grant a true, willing spirit, I pray.

I'll then teach transgressors to keep Your ways,
And, so, sinners will turn back to You.
Redeem me from blood-guilt, then I will praise,
And I'll sing of Your righteousness, too.

You won't take delight in a sacrifice—
If you did, I would readily give.
Nor will You be pleased with burnt offerings nice;
What You want is an offering that lives.

A spirit that's broken and humble must
Be the sacrifice right in Your eyes.
A broken and contrite, true heart with trust
Is the one that You will not despise.

Though you have not seen [Jesus Christ], you love him. Though you do not now see him, you believe in him and rejoice with joy that is inexpressible and filled with glory, obtaining the outcome of your faith, the salvation of your souls.   *(I Peter 1:8-9)*

And let the peace of Christ rule in your hearts, to which indeed you were called in one body. And be thankful.   *(Colossians 3:15)*

May the God of hope fill you with all joy and peace in believing, so that by the power of the Holy Spirit you may abound in hope.   *(Romans 15:13)*

Claiming a New Name

It's God's character that we denote by His Name,
And we call Him our Rock, for He's always the same.
But our God can change us, so we are as He aimed,
And then when we're transformed, it's like we've been renamed.

As we see in God's Word, Abram, Jacob and Saul
Did receive their new names when they answered God's call.
God's been calling me, now, through my forty-five years,
Yet depression and worry enveloped my ears.

Yes, in fact, you could say those things characterized me,
So, my name was "Depression, Anxiety."
Since, though sometimes they'd lift, they would always come back,
I was blind to God's blessings and saw only lack.

Yet, my God and His blessings were always assured;
Like the sky, they were just by life's clouds oft obscured.
Since Christ rose from the dead, I can trust that, in sum:
When the sun's overcast, it is not overcome!

Hence, my God and His Son, though unseen, are not gone—
They are here, whether I'm in life's night or life's dawn.
And God's promises mean that He's not simply "there":
He is carrying me, and He answers each prayer.

And God's taught me my value is not what I do
Or how I measure up to all those that I knew.
God did give me my gifts; my sins He erased.
I can rest: all the glory is His for His grace.

Now, when Christ came to Paul, it was with blinding light,
But this faith's come to me as a slow-clearing sight.
Yet, the end's still the same, for our God still transforms,
Giving joy in His Name and peace through life's storms.

My brain's chemicals may still just come and then go;
I may feel more up now, and then down—this I know.
But depression's long hold and anxiety's claim
Have been broken by God, who gives me a new name!

For my mindset's a choice, not determined by chance;
I choose Christ as my Rock, so I'm freed to advance.
I delight in my God, trust His Will, find release;
The new name I now claim, then, is His "Joy and Peace"!

The Work of Worship

(for Pastor Laurey Berteig, Westminster Chapel Choir Director, based on his favorite scriptures)

Come and sing to the LORD a new song;
Oh sing to the LORD, all the earth!
Tell His wonderful deeds all day long;
Declare His true glory and worth.

To the nations, proclaim Him as great.
God is to be feared and then praised.
There is nothing He didn't create—
Tear down all the idols you've raised.

Where He dwells there is beauty and might,
Great splendor and majesty, too.
In His courts, I will offer what's right
And give Him the glory He's due.

"But, my Lord, I can't stay in Your court—
At church or within my own soul.
Must routine cut my worship time short?
Explain to me worship's true role."

"You can worship Me all of the time.
My child, lift your eyes and you'll see:
You face hills, not to boast in the climb,
But so you will find help in Me.

"King David did follow My heart
And worshipped in line with My will.
Humble trust placed in Me was his part;
My promise I then did fulfill:

"Both a shepherd and sheep in My flock—
'Twas I who established his throne.
He cried out, 'You're my Father, my Rock;
I've done not one thing on my own.'

"So, acknowledge Me in all your ways,
And I will, then, make your paths straight.
Needing counsel? Then, here's your true praise:
To lean on My wisdom and wait.

"While you're waiting, do you feel ignored?
Remember the truth you have heard:
The Creator of all—I'm the Lord!
I faint or not know? That's absurd!

"When you're weary, My power I give.
No might? Your small strength I increase.
Wait for Me: that's the real way to live;
You'll walk, run, and soar without cease.

"I am with you; I'll help you to stand.
Fear not, and do not be dismayed.
I uphold with My righteous right hand,
So worshipers won't be afraid.

"And I hold your right hand now as well—
Your strong hand, yet it is still weak.
'So, fear not, your God helps you,' I tell.
You'll find not one foe when you seek."

"You're my light and salvation, my Lord,
So why should I be all afraid?
I am bound to You by a strong cord:
You carry each one You have made."

"When you come to Me, you will find rest,
So pray without ceasing to Me,
And give thanks when you make your request,
Thus, keeping yourself worry-free.

"And My peace will then guard heart and mind
Beyond what you can comprehend.
Then, when worry is left far behind,
Just think on the things I commend."

"Lord, on You, thus, my mind will remain;
In peace that is perfect I'm kept,
For I trust in the One who'll sustain.
I'm safe, because You've never slept."

"Both the sun and the moon I direct;
By day or by night, they won't harm.
Worship Me as the One who'll protect
Your movements and life from alarm.

"I'll not leave you, nor will I forsake.
You lead in My church, and I'm there.
None can thwart all that you undertake
When it's My own will that's your prayer.

"I'm your heavenly Father, so pray
And ask that My will would be done.
Bring your cares and your needs for the day;
Just ask—I'll provide for each one.

"Now, you also need Me to forgive;
Forgive those who sin against you.
Yes, temptations will come where you live,
But ask Me, and I'll bring you through.

"In My Son, I have given the way,
The truth, and the life that's your light.
I'll complete my good work at that Day
When Jesus returns to your sight."

"Though impossible that is with man,
Lord, I will believe what You've said.
You'll accomplish all things in Your plan;
I trust You, for You've raised the dead!

"And You've raised me from my death in sin;
Your Spirit lives in me to save.
Now, I live here by faith that's within:
By trust in the One that You gave.

"Lord, You're for me, so who can oppose?
You've given me all things, and more!
My true worship's the way that I chose
My heart, soul, and mind to be Yours."

"In life's trials, child, do not forget:
Through Jesus, you do rise above,
For there's nothing you'll face or have met
That separates you from My love."

"I will work, Lord, with all of my heart
For You—not for men or for me,
Since I've known this great truth from the start:
The One that I worship I'll see!"

For I, the LORD your God, hold your right hand; it is I who say to you, "Fear not, I am the one who helps you." *(Isaiah 41:13)*

See also—Psalm 96:1-8, Isaiah 40:27-31, Psalm 121, Romans 8:31-32, 37-39, Matthew 6:9-13

It is the LORD who goes before you. He will be with you; he will not leave you or forsake you. Do not fear or be dismayed.   *(Deuteronomy 31:8)*

As a father shows compassion to his children, so the LORD shows compassion to those who fear him.   *(Psalm 103:13)*

The eternal God is your dwelling place, and underneath are the everlasting arms.
                                                                                     (Deuteronomy 33:27a)

[God] will wipe away every tear from their eyes, and death shall be no more, neither shall there be mourning, nor crying, nor pain anymore, for the former things have passed away.
                                                                                     (Revelation 21:4)

See also—Genesis 1:26-27, II Corinthians 1:3-4, Romans 8:29, John 15:15, Romans 8:32

The Presence of Comfort
(for Patty Berteig)

"My child, I made the loved ones you've lost,
So I alone know bereavement's true cost:
The parts of you they took when they went,
Each piece of your soul that from you was rent.

"I know why grief so devastates, too,
That gaping black hole that pierces you through:
For in My image each person's made,
A ray of My truth and glory displayed—

"A ray unique in time and in space,
So no human can its beauty replace.
No earthly thing can heal grief, of course;
I offer, not substitutes, but the Source!

"Each precious good they'd shown and begun
Is ever in Me, My Spirit and Son.
Grief's cure is then what's always been true—
The answer for all: that 'I am with you.'

"I am 'the God of all comfort,' so
I see and console each sorrow you know.
And how I fill the void griefs create
Is found in the ways in which I relate:

"A parent's left—your life's faithful guide;
I'm Father to you, and I will provide.
I keep you safe from all that could harm,
And hold you in everlasting, strong arms.

"A sibling's gone, who watched as you grew;
My Son calls you 'Brother'—He's family, too!
He knew and loved you, still in your sin;
He gave up His life, so I'd take you in.

"A friend has died—your lives so did blend;
Your Savior, My Son, as well calls you 'Friend.'
He shares with you and walks right beside,
So close: He's the One in whom you abide!

"The time has come that death did you part;
It feels like the end has torn out your heart.
You were 'one flesh;' though death cut that cord,
You're 'one spirit' with your undying Lord.

"Your child was taken—anguish defined;
To give up My Son was what I designed
To rescue you from death's bitter sting,
And, with Him, I'll give you every good thing.

"And 'all good things' means all that you need—
In grief or in joy: all paths where I lead.
You've comfort now, because I am here;
When I take you Home, I'll wipe every tear!"

77

When you pass through the waters, I will be with you; and through the rivers, they shall not overwhelm you; when you walk through fire you shall not be burned, and the flame shall not consume you. *(Isaiah 43:2)*

For God alone, O my soul, wait in silence, for my hope is from him. He only is my rock and my salvation, my fortress; I shall not be shaken. On God rests my salvation and my glory; my mighty rock, my refuge is God. Trust in him at all times, O people; pour out your heart before him; God is a refuge for us. *(Psalm 62:5-8)*

I waited patiently for the LORD; he inclined to me and heard my cry. He drew me up from the pit of destruction, out of the miry bog, and set my feet upon a rock, making my steps secure. He put a new song in my mouth, a song of praise to our God. Many will see and fear, and put their trust in the LORD. *(Psalm 40:1-3)*

Arise, shine, for your light has come, and the glory of the LORD has risen upon you. For behold, darkness shall cover the earth, and thick darkness the peoples; but the LORD will arise upon you, and his glory will be seen upon you. *(Isaiah 60:1-2)*

See also—Psalm 27:7-8, 27:4; Colossians 3:15-16, Isaiah 43:18-19, Job 23:10, Psalm 63:1, 7-8

The Walk of Worship

(for Arlene Finley, Director of Worship, Westminster Chapel)

"Oh, come unto Me, all who toil;
It is I who will give to you rest.
Then, taking My yoke, learn from Me,
For My burden is light through each test."

"Lord, hear when my voice cries aloud;
Then, have mercy upon me and speak!
And, Lord, You have said, 'Seek My face.'
Says my heart: 'Lord, Your face I will seek.'

"There's one thing I ask and pursue:
In the house of the Lord may I dwell
To gaze on the beauty of God;
Then, about Your great glory I'll tell."

"My child, let My peace rule your heart.
Let My word in you dwell and then teach.
With psalms, hymns and spiritual songs,
Thus, the hearts of My people you'll reach."

"Your love is much better than life,
So my lips will sing forth Your true praise.
My hands I will lift in Your name,
And I'll bless You for all of my days."

"I'm pleased with your worship and praise,
Since I'm seeking for people who will
Now worship in spirit and truth,
For they thereby true worship fulfill."

"A living, pure sacrifice: thus
I'll present, now, my body to You,
For this is the right way to serve
And to spiritually worship You, too.

"For You, Lord, alone I will wait,
For my hope comes from You, not my dreams.
You're fortress, salvation—my rock,
So I shall not be moved by what 'seems.'"

"On Me, child, your glory depends,
As, on Me, your salvation does rest.
Before Me, pour out your whole heart;
I'm your refuge—I do what is best."

"O Father, You are my own God.
In this trial, I'm seeking Your hand.
My soul truly thirsts, my flesh faints
As I travel this dry, weary land."

"Fear not, for you're one I've redeemed;
I have called you by name, you are mine.
This fire can never consume;
It can only induce you to shine.

"Behold, I am doing new things;
Do not dwell on the things from of old.
I know all the ways that you take;
When I've tried you, you will be as gold."

"With patience, for You I did wait,
And my cry unto You has been heard.
You lifted me out of the pit;
All my steps have been firmly secured."

"I've given a new song to you,
So your praise will draw men unto Me.
Each trial will bring its own song;
I work all for your good—you will see."

"My Help, I will sing and rejoice
As I rest in the shade of Your wings.
Your hand ever carries and holds,
And so ever to You my soul clings."

"Feel blind? You can know I will lead,
And the darkness I'll turn to daybreak.
From rough, I will make level ground:
All these things, and I do not forsake.

"Though even the mountains may leave,
And perhaps all the hills run away,
My love for you won't be removed,
And My covenant always will stay.

"Arise, now, and shine—your light's come,
And on you is My glory so bright.
Yes, darkness may cover the earth,
But, in you, all will see My true light!"

The LORD is my chosen portion and my cup; you hold my lot. The lines have fallen for me in pleasant places; indeed, I have a beautiful inheritance.   *(Psalm 16:5-6)*

"The LORD is my portion," says my soul, "therefore I will hope in him."   *(Lamentations 3:24)*

I cry to you, O LORD; I say, "You are my refuge, my portion in the land of the living."
                                                                                 (Psalm 142:5)

And [Jesus] said to all, "If anyone would come after me, let him deny himself and take up his cross daily and follow me. For whoever would save his life will lose it, but whoever loses his life for my sake will save it."   *(Luke 9:23-24)*

Whom have I in heaven but you? And there is nothing on earth that I desire besides you. My flesh and my heart may fail, but God is the strength of my heart and my portion forever.
                                                                                 (Psalm 73:25-26)

See also—John 15:4-5

Abiding at His Feet

(based in part on Luke 10:38-42)

When Jesus had come to a certain small town,
It was Martha who asked Him to stay.
Her sister named Mary then sat herself down
At Christ's feet just to hear what He'd say.

But Martha, distracted by serving alone,
Came to Jesus and cried, "Don't you care?
My sister has left me to work on my own.
You must tell her the workload to share."

Then Jesus said, "Martha, you fret at so much,
There's just one thing that's needed, I say,
And Mary did choose the good portion—it's such
That it shall not be taken away."

What had Mary chosen that no one could take?
In the psalms and the prophets we've read:
"The Lord is my portion: the choice I did make."
"I will hope in and trust Him," they said.

This world that is fallen has much that can leave:
Health and wealth, friends and kin, strength and peace.
But if, losing all, to the Lord we will cleave,
We'll have life that will only increase.

"Abide now in Me as I'm also in you;"
Jesus taught, "In this way, you'll bear fruit."
Apart from our Lord, there's no good we can do;
We serve truly as Christ's our pursuit.

Abiding in Christ was what Mary had done,
As the branch must abide in the vine.
So, since she had chosen priority one,
She could say, "I am His; He is mine."

When we say, "Whom have I in heaven but You?
I desire not one earthly toy,"
For life and forever—eternity through—
We'll have God as our portion and joy!

I appeal to you therefore, brothers, by the mercies of God, to present your bodies as a living sacrifice, holy and acceptable to God, which is your spiritual worship. *(Romans 12:1)*

But I do not account my life of any value nor as precious to myself, if only I may finish my course and the ministry that I received from the Lord Jesus, to testify to the gospel of the grace of God. *(Acts 20:24)*

"I am the vine; you are the branches. Whoever abides in me and I in him, he it is that bears much fruit, for apart from me you can do nothing." *(John 15:5)*

To [his saints] God chose to make known how great among the Gentiles are the riches of the glory of this mystery, which is Christ in you, the hope of glory. Him we proclaim, warning everyone and teaching everyone with all wisdom, that we may present everyone mature in Christ. For this I toil, struggling with all his energy that he powerfully works within me. *(Colossians 1:27-29)*

Course Commendation

(for Margaret Luke, based on her favorite scriptures)

"Your course is not yet finished, but
I see you're running well.
Your life and work have pleased Me much—
Beyond what words can tell.

"Before you ever worked for Me,
I gave My Son for you.
You're precious, loved and honored, child,
Apart from aught you do.

"You know that you are not your own;
I paid the highest price,
And so, you glorify Me as
A living sacrifice.

"As such, you count your life but loss,
A freed and willing slave.
You aim to finish now your course:
The ministry I gave.

"My witness, you do testify
About the gospel's grace,
And, bearing fruit through Me, you run
With patience your own race.

"And I delight in how you teach:
In love, with motives pure.
You speak with all My wisdom, so
That saints may be mature.

"I know you toil, and struggle, too;
You know that it's My pow'r.
My Spirit thus performs My will
As you submit each hour.

"You're saved by Love—in love, you serve.
Your life has sung this tune:
The mystery that's Christ in you,
The hope of glory—soon!"

Found, Fruitful, and Found Faithful

(for Dr. Gary Gulbranson on his 20th Anniversary as Senior Pastor of Westminster Chapel, 6-16-13)

"Bring your thirst to the waters—they're free!
Come, ye starving and bankrupt, be fed!
All who labor, now come unto Me;
Come, and taste living water and bread!

"When you taste, you will see that I'm good.
When it's I that's your refuge, you're blest.
Take My yoke, learn of Me—free of 'should.'
Nestle under My wings and find rest!"

"I have come and been crucified with Christ:
It is Christ who lives in me, not I.
So, I now live as one sacrificed:
A life hidden with Jesus on high.

"I'm a young man; how can I stay pure?
It's Your Word that will guard me and guide.
With its lamp for my feet, my path's sure:
Kept from sin by Your words deep inside.

"You have said, 'Seek My face.' Lord, I seek!
Yes, in fact, one thing only I ask:
May Your beauty I see. Then, I'll speak
Of Your grace that's my strength. What's my
   task?"

"Not that I am your choice, but you're Mine;
I've ordained you to go and bear fruit.
Dwell in Me as a branch in the Vine;
You will thrive as My words do take root.

"Do your best to present yourself approved;
Paint aright the full truth of My Word.
Then, you'll not be ashamed nor be moved,
Speaking just what from Me you have heard."

"How I love Your great law, for it's sweet
As I meditate through every day.
I am wiser than others I meet,
For I study and keep Your right way.

"I will cleanse self from what is unclean;
Lord, please use me, for I'm set apart.
Let me go to Your harvest and glean,
Since I hurt for the lost on Your heart."

"I will give you My Word like the snow,
Which gives water to nourish and feed.
It's from My mouth through yours, so you'll know:
Never void; it will always succeed!"

"I've learned much, but, O God, let my speech
Now be only of Christ crucified.
By Your pow'r, not my wisdom, I preach
To stir faith that draws men to Your side."

"A meek servant, you're just like My Son;
You have had Jesus' mindset for years.
Persevere—there's a new race to run:
You are called now to serve through your tears."

"My soul clings to the dust where she's laid;
Give me life as You've said that you would!
My soul melts—she's with you, but I've stayed.
Give me strength, if, indeed, You are good!

"I will cling to Your promise and hand;
Don't allow me to be put to shame!
I'll still run in the way You command;
Please, just help me to trust in Your Name!

"Let my eyes open wide to behold
Even more than You've shown in past years.
You have tried me, now make me as gold;
Make a prism from each of my tears!"

"Child, I know all the way that you take.
You've responded each time that I call.
I'm the One that you need when earth quakes:
I am here; I have heard; you won't fall!

"Still My steadfast, true love has not ceased;
I am faithful to those that I choose.
Now, the ways you can serve have increased:
Broken vessels are those that I use!

"With your roots in My Word as I've willed,
You're a tree that is planted by streams.
You obeyed, though your hopes had been killed,
And you gave Me your pain to redeem."

"Lord, my trust is in You—I've no fear.
I have peace, because You're my pursuit.
I'm not anxious, though heat and drought near,
For, in You, I will always bear fruit.

"I look forward to fruit at each stage,
Full of sap and still green though mature.
Yet more truth I'll declare as I age:
You're my Rock, and Your Word will endure."

"You were born into Me: life made new;
Your joy grew as you trusted through strife.
Loving Me, stand each test till they're through,
And I'll give you the crown of life.

"Fight for Me, keep the faith, run your race,
For there's laid up for you yet a crown.
You are freed to take up divine grace
Every time that you lay your life down.

"I'm well-pleased with your work and your trust.
Through your trials, you have been made whole.
Above all, I am Love, so it's just
Your true good that is always My goal!"

Do your best to present yourself to God as one approved, a worker who has no need to be ashamed, rightly handling the word of truth.   *(II Timothy 2:15)*

The righteous flourish like the palm tree and grow like a cedar in Lebanon…They still bear fruit in old age; they are ever full of sap and green, to declare that the Lord is upright; he is my rock, and there is no unrighteousness in him.   *(Psalm 92:12, 14-15)*

See also—Isaiah 55:1, Psalm 119:9, 25, 28, 31-32; II Timothy 2:21, Isaiah 55:10-11
I Corinthians 2:1-5, Psalm 75:3, James 1:12, II Timothy 4:7-8, James 1:2-4, Romans 8:28

Rejoice always, pray without ceasing, give thanks in all circumstances; for this is the will of God in Christ Jesus for you. *(I Thessalonians 5:16-18)*

The LORD is near to all who call on him, to all who call on him in truth. *(Psalm 145:18)*

But I will hope continually and will praise you yet more and more. My mouth will tell of your righteous acts, of your deeds of salvation all the day, for their number is past my knowledge. *(Psalm 71:14-15)*

Then you will call upon me and come and pray to me, and I will hear you. You will seek me and find me, when you seek me with all your heart. *(Jeremiah 29:12-13)*

Offer to God a sacrifice of thanksgiving, and perform your vows to the Most High, and call upon me in the day of trouble; I will deliver you, and you shall glorify me. *(Psalm 50:14-15)*

Seeking God, Finding Joy

(outline based on Psalm 105:1-5)

What now can I write that I haven't before?
And how can I fight this despair one time more?
What truth can I learn that I haven't yet found?
Which weapon will give me the victory this round?

So much truth based on Scripture has flowed from my pen,
Yet I can't see its light when I read it again.
For the eyes of my heart have been blinded anew
As the comfort once grasped now no longer feels true.

Yes, I'm doubting my God, so I'm tossed like a wave.
Will I let the storm win, or find faith that will save?
Though this night blinds my eyes, will I trust what
   I've heard?
For the Scripture says faith comes from hearing
   Christ's Word.

I recall that God's Word is the Spirit's sharp sword,
And I read in a psalm, "Oh give thanks to the LORD."
With this first short command, that Sword cuts to the heart,
For thanksgiving is how my sure victory will start.

When depression comes in, then out gratitude goes,
And I miss even blessings right under my nose.
God's design will not leave joy's first key up to chance,
So, He tells me, "Give thanks throughout each
   circumstance."

Circumstances have changed, but my God stays the same,
Thus, He urges me, second, to call on His name.
When I call on the Lord, I've true hope, since He's near,
And He's promised He'll answer and save, for He hears.

To make known the Lord's deeds among men, next I'm told,
For a focus on God and His works makes faith bold.
When I then sing to God and my voice to Him raise,
He'll exchange my faint spirit for the garment of praise!

When I speak, I'm to tell of all God's wondrous deeds,
Thus reminding myself He can meet all my needs.
To delight and to glory in God's holy name
Then relieves all the pressure to earn my own fame.

I am one who seeks God—let my heart now rejoice,
For He's found by all those who make Him their first choice.
"Seek the LORD and His strength," by the psalmist I'm taught;
Christ confirmed that apart from Him I can do naught.

Also, "Seek the LORD's presence continually;"
If I seek His face here, soon His face I shall see!
Last, "Remember God's judgments, His miracles, too"—
He has saved in the past; He'll again bring me through!

God's prescription for joy lies in these ten commands,
And there's strength to obey when I rest in His hands.
When I focus on God, hope shines bright—troubles dim,
For my help will come only, yet always, from Him!

And Mary said, "My soul magnifies the Lord, and my spirit rejoices in God my Savior, for he has looked on the humble estate of his servant. For behold, from now on all generations will call me blessed; for he who is mighty has done great things for me, and holy is his name."

(Luke 1:46-49)

But as [Joseph] considered these things, behold, an angel of the Lord appeared to him in a dream, saying, "Joseph, son of David, do not fear to take Mary as your wife, for that which is conceived in her is from the Holy Spirit. She will bear a son, and you shall call his name Jesus, for he will save his people from their sins."

(Matthew 1:20-21)

[Simeon] took [the child Jesus] up in his arms and blessed God and said, "Lord, now you are letting your servant depart in peace, according to your word; for my eyes have seen your salvation that you have prepared in the presence of all peoples, a light for revelation to the Gentiles, and for glory to your people Israel."

(Luke 2:28-32)

For to us a child is born, to us a son is given; and the government shall be upon his shoulder, and his name shall be called Wonderful Counselor, Mighty God, Everlasting Father, Prince of Peace.

(Isaiah 9:6)

The Cast of Christmas

The first Christmas pageant involved many roles;
We're so versed in their acts, we've forgotten their souls.
So, how do these characters play their new parts?
And what truth can we learn from the state of their
   hearts?

First, Gabriel's greeting made Mary distraught,
Yet she heeded his message and charge to "Fear not."
She said—based on faith, not on what she could see—
"I'm God's servant; thus let it be done unto me."

Next, praise and rejoicing in God she expressed,
And she claimed, "They will call me, not great, but just
   blessed,
For God has now done these great things with His might.
I say Holy's His name, and in Him I delight!"

An angel announced, then, in Joseph's true dream:
"Do not fear to take Mary—things aren't as they seem.
God's Spirit is how Mary's babe was conceived,
For her son is your Savior." And Joseph believed!

He trusted the Lord with his spouse and his life,
So he took pregnant Mary as his wedded wife.
Yes, Joseph obeyed what the Lord did command,
And he called this babe Jesus as God aptly planned.

An angel appeared to some shepherds that night,
And the glory of God 'round them filled them with fright.
"Fear not," said the angel, "I tell of great joy:
In a manger's your Savior: a swaddling-clothed boy."

Unlikely it seemed, yet they trusted and went,
And so found the great joy which the angel had meant.
No presents to bring, but these shepherds told all.
And in sharing their news, they fulfilled their high call.

Now, Simeon came, for his faith had sufficed
To believe that his eyes would yet see the Lord's Christ.
This righteous man waited and hoped in God's word;
Thus, he saw God's salvation just as he had heard.

The prophetess Anna had old age to bear,
Yet she stayed in the temple in fasting and prayer.
She gave thanks to God when babe Jesus was brought
And then witnessed to all who redemption had sought.

Then, wise men were searching, so they saw the star.
Waiting, ready to follow, they came from afar.
Their hearts were receptive to life-altering news,
So they traveled to worship the King of the Jews.

But Herod the king in his pride was concerned
To remove this new king of whose birth he had learned.
Pretending to worship, he did as he willed:
Hence, in rage, gave the order that babies be killed.

The priests and the scribes knew the birthplace when
   asked,
For they'd studied the prophets just as they'd been
   tasked.
But they did not worship, and they did not go,
For their hearts did reject what their minds had to know.

The star led the wise men to this divine boy;
When they saw, they rejoiced with exceeding great joy!
They gave to Him gifts of pure myrrh and of gold,
And their hearts gave Him worship—their Savior foretold.

Thus, most of this cast their true Christ recognized—
They believed in God's Word, and it opened their eyes.
A few, though, were blinded by pride or by greed—
Thought themselves and this earth gave them all they
   could need.

But who was the hero—the star of this play?
It is Jesus, this King we still worship today.
This babe is the King come to take away sin.
He has conquered the grave—now will you let Him in?

He's Wonderful Counselor—give Him your heart;
Let the Mighty God fight for you—Christ takes your part.
Everlasting Father—find rest as His child;
He's the Prince of true Peace—come and be reconciled!

"O afflicted one, storm-tossed and not comforted, behold, I will set your stones in antimony, and lay your foundations with sapphires. I will make your pinnacles of agate, your gates of carbuncles, and all your wall of precious stones."   *(Isaiah 54:11-12)*

One thing have I asked of the LORD, that will I seek after: that I may dwell in the house of the LORD all the days of my life, to gaze upon the beauty of the LORD and to inquire in his temple.

(Psalm 27:4)

Have you not known? Have you not heard? The LORD is the everlasting God, the Creator of the ends of the earth. He does not faint or grow weary; his understanding is unsearchable. He gives power to the faint, and to him who has no might he increases strength. Even youths shall faint and be weary, and young men shall fall exhausted; but they who wait for the LORD shall renew their strength; they shall mount up with wings like eagles; they shall run and not be weary; they shall walk and not faint.   *(Isaiah 40:28-31)*

And your ancient ruins shall be rebuilt; you shall raise up the foundations of many generations; you shall be called the repairer of the breach, the restorer of streets to dwell in.   *(Isaiah 58:12)*

Nevertheless, I [the psalmist] am continually with you; you hold my right hand. You guide me with your counsel, and afterward you will receive me to glory.   *(Psalm 73:23-24)*

See also—Deuteronomy 33:27a, Matthew 7:24, Psalm 37:4, II Corinthians 12:8-10, Isaiah 40:26

Delight in a Dear Disciple

(For Holly Messinger, based on her favorite scriptures)

"O, afflicted one, by great storms you've been tossed,
Needing comfort when none was on earth.
You are found in Me, though you've often felt lost;
In My sight, you're a jewel of great worth.

"Your young life faced gales, angry waves, shifting sands:
Full of turmoil and pain and alarms.
But you're dwelling now in My kind, gentle hands,
Held in My everlasting, strong arms.

"You have built your life on the rock of My Word,
And in Me you have taken delight.
Your desires I'll grant—your one prayer I have heard:
I will show you My beauty and might.

"I have also heard your requests for relief
From the thorns in your heart and your flesh.
Though I've let them stay, I provide in your grief:
Grace sufficient and strength ever fresh.

"For the sake of Christ, thus you're resting content,
Though insulted and suffering and weak.
Since you trust My plan, you accept what I've sent;
It's the power of Christ that you seek.

"Then, you lift your eyes to see all I have made,
And you hear Me call stars out by name.
If you tire and faint, I will come to your aid,
And My power and strength you'll proclaim.

"You'll renew your strength as you hope in your Lord;
As you wait, you shall mount up with wings.
You shall run—not tired, but with power restored;
When you walk, you'll not faint: you will sing.

"And your ancient ruins I vow to rebuild.
The foundations of wreckage you'll raise.
You'll repair the breaches as I've always willed,
For, My child, you're a woman who prays!

"You have walked with Me, and I've stayed by your side.
I will hold your right hand through all strife.
I'll provide, protect; I will lead you and guide,
Then receive you to Glory and Life!"

For your Maker is your husband, the LORD of hosts is his name; and the Holy One of Israel is your Redeemer, the God of the whole earth he is called. *(Isaiah 54:5)*

I myself will be the shepherd of my sheep, and I myself will make them lie down, declares the Lord GOD. I will seek the lost, and I will bring back the strayed, and I will bind up the injured, and I will strengthen the weak… *(Ezekiel 34:15-16a)*

The LORD is merciful and gracious, slow to anger and abounding in steadfast love. *(Psalm 103:8)*

"Do you not believe that I [Jesus] am in the Father and the Father is in me? The words that I say to you I do not speak on my own authority, but the Father who dwells in me does his works." *(John 14:10)*

See also—Isaiah 49:15-16, Psalm 103:13, Isaiah 49:5-6, Malachi 3:6, I John 4:7-10

A Record of Relentless Love

I'd heard, "We love God for He first loved us"
But did not really know He loved me.
Instead, I felt judged and condemned, and thus
Lived on shackled though told I was free.

I thought I was doing just what God asks.
I knew scriptures and hymns so was sure;
Knew not I was serving with all my tasks
An Old Testament caricature.

"A God of great wrath"—this you've heard before—
So He seemed in Old Testament's age.
"A God of true love," then proceeds the lore,
Since Christ came and turned history's page.

Yet history's not like a book with leaves;
It's unbroken: a banner of love,
Which tells how our God's every action weaves
All together with care from above.

With Adam and Eve, God did walk at first;
He desired a connection with man.
Thus, knowing the Serpent would do his worst,
Before time, God had made His whole plan.

So, God made a promise to Abraham;
Out of Israel, a nation He made.
He showed them Himself as the great I AM,
And, in Egypt, deliverance displayed.

God's law was like love etched in stone,
 which gave
Them prosperity's path for their land.
God cherished His people as though engraved
With His love on the palm of His hand.

As Father with love for His precious child,
As a Husband desiring His bride,
As Shepherd who seeks a lost sheep run wild:
Thus, God claimed that His love did abide.

King David explained, "God is gracious, kind;
Slow to anger, He loves without end—
Forgives when we've flouted what He'd designed."
God, then, primed them for Love to descend.

Isaiah the prophet good news foretold;
The Messiah would sound forth God's call:
God wants every nation within His fold—
Now the Light of the world shines for all.

Christ came and spoke only the Father's words;
He did naught but the Father's own will.
God's love, then, of which they had always heard
Was poured out onto Calvary's hill.

In Christ, there is no condemnation: thus
The New Testament anthem now rings;
God spared not His Son—gave Him up for us—
With Him, graciously gives us all things!

Past, present, and future—our God's the same:
He is love—was, and always will be.
And, grasping this truth, I can now proclaim:
I love God, since I know He loves me!

The LORD is near to the brokenhearted and saves the crushed in spirit. *(Psalm 34:18)*

You have kept count of my tossings; put my tears in your bottle. Are they not in your book? *(Psalm 56:8)*

And I will lead the blind in a way that they do not know, in paths that they have not known I will guide them. I will turn the darkness before them into light, the rough places into level ground. These are the things I do, and I do not forsake them. *(Isaiah 42:16)*

The Spirit of the Lord GOD is upon me, because the LORD has anointed me to bring good news to the poor; he has sent me to bind up the brokenhearted...to grant to those who mourn in Zion—to give them a beautiful headdress instead of ashes, the oil of gladness instead of mourning, the garment of praise instead of a faint spirit; that they may be called oaks of righteousness, the planting of the LORD, that he may be glorified. *(Isaiah 61:1a, 3)*

Who shall separate us from the love of Christ? Shall tribulation, or distress, or persecution, or famine, or nakedness, or danger, or sword?... No, in all these things we are more than conquerors through him who loved us. *(Romans 8:35, 37)*

See also—Isaiah 46:3-4, Psalm 139:7-9, 11-12; Psalm 30:5, Psalm 9:9-10, Isaiah 60:1

Promises for the Path of Pain

(for Arlene Finley)

Your life has been turned upside down overnight.
Every day from now on is an uphill fight.
You face a new future that's drastically changed;
Hopeful plans must be tragically rearranged.

You're wondering why this has all been allowed,
And you can't find a light in the looming cloud.
It feels as if God has just left—isn't there;
And you ask, "Will God help? Does He even care?"

Your Heavenly Father then speaks through His Word
With the most tender voice that you've ever heard:
" Child, first, be assured you are seen—your
    pain's known,
For My eyes never leave those I call My own.

"I hear as you call, even when you ask, 'Why?'
For My ears still attend to your every cry.
To hearts that are broken I'm specially near,
And when grief overflows, I record each tear.

"No trial can alter that I am with you.
From the womb to the grave, I will bear you through.
There's never a moment you're not in My care;
There's no place pain can take you that I'm not there.

"All 'round you is darkness, but I see the way,
For to Me deepest night is as bright as day.
You're now flying blind, but I'm here by your side,
And I hold your right hand. Do not fear; I'll guide.

"I'll turn all the darkness before you to light,
And rough ground will be leveled before your sight.
You'll not be consumed by this fire's great heat,
And you're not overwhelmed by the floods you meet.

"I'll bind up your wounds—they won't tear you apart—
And I'll heal and make whole all your broken heart.
What seemed like your rock has been scattered
    like sand,
But, child, I'm your true Rock, and on Me you'll stand.

"My peace and real joy will soon sadness displace.
In the meantime, I give all-sufficient grace.
For wisdom and strength you have only to ask;
You'll receive all you need for each daunting task.

"Your old life is gone, but I'm doing new things:
I make paths in this wilderness, desert springs.
Drawn up from this pit, you will sing a new song—
This can be, since My strength ever makes you strong.

"The God of all comfort am I as you mourn.
I give beauty for ashes and hope reborn.
The heavy of spirit don garments of praise;
I exchange their deep mourning for joy that stays.

"My presence and promises free the oppressed.
As you come unto Me, I will give you rest.
You're more than a conqueror, because you are Mine.
As My light ends this night, you'll arise and shine!"

O Israel, hope in the LORD! For with the LORD there is steadfast love, and with him is plentiful redemption.   *(Psalm 130:7)*

Blessed be the God and Father of our Lord Jesus Christ! According to his great mercy, he has caused us to be born again to a living hope through the resurrection of Jesus Christ from the dead, to an inheritance that is imperishable, undefiled, and unfading, kept in heaven for you, who by God's power are being guarded through faith for a salvation ready to be revealed in the last time.   *(I Peter 1:3-5)*

Therefore, preparing your minds for action, and being sober-minded, set your hope fully on the grace that will be brought to you at the revelation of Jesus Christ.   *(I Peter 1:13)*

Beloved, we are God's children now, and what we will be has not yet appeared; but we know that when he appears we shall be like him, because we shall see him as he is.   *(I John 3:2)*

And not only the creation, but we ourselves, who have the firstfruits of the Spirit, groan inwardly as we wait eagerly for adoption as sons, the redemption of our bodies. For in this hope we were saved. Now hope that is seen is not hope. For who hopes for what he sees? But if we hope for what we do not see, we wait for it with patience.   *(Romans 8:23-25)*

See also—Colossians 1:27, Colossians 1:4-5, Titus 2:13, Ephesians 1:16-18, I Peter 1:8-9

Expecting Eternity

"Now hope in the LORD and His promised word."
This command from psalmists God's people heard,
For the LORD their God, then, had just begun
To love and redeem every downcast one.

The prophet despaired when God seemed unkind,
But his hope returned when he called to mind
How God's love won't end—it is always there—
And how every day He gives faithful care.

Before Jesus came, all God's people knew
Was to hope in Him, but they'd little clue
To redemption's goal; they knew not that, thus,
The hope of true glory is Christ in us!

But I know the truth of my future, yet
 I lose hope so often as I forget.
Then, it seems my suffering will last too long,
So now, let me pause, and I'll hear hope's song:

Paul calls it a mystery but gives hints
That in heaven's stored our inheritance.
We are "born again to a living hope,"
Which can't ever fade and is vast in scope.

Christ rose and ascended, and His return
Is the "blessed hope": that for which we yearn.
So, our hope's set fully upon the grace
We know we'll receive when we see His face.

We'll be resurrected, just like our Lord:
Bodies glorified, perfect souls restored.
An eternal joy that's with Him enthralled:
Yes, this is the hope unto which we're called.

We're groaning along with creation's pain;
We await redemption, but not in vain.
We rejoice in Him that we cannot see
By faith that is placed in His guarantee.

Now, hope lifts our eyes, and it lightens hearts
As we live to follow the course God charts.
We endure with patience here while we roam,
For hope still reminds, "This is not your home!"

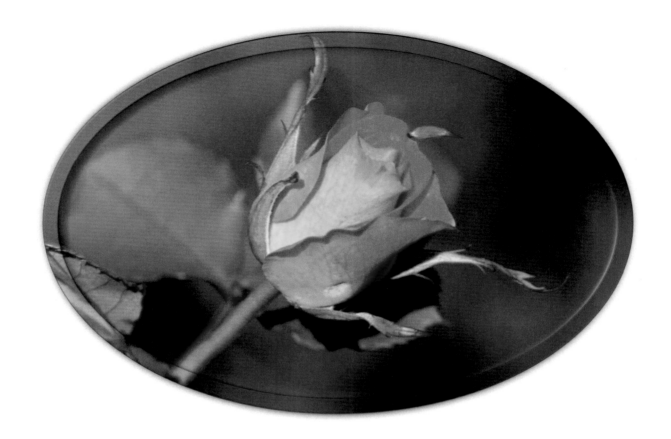

But now thus says the LORD, he who created you, O Jacob, he who formed you, O Israel: "Fear not, for I have redeemed you; I have called you by name, you are mine." *(Isaiah 43:1)*

"In the same way, let your light shine before others, so that they may see your good works and give glory to your Father who is in heaven." *(Matthew 5:16)*

What do you have that you did not receive? If then you received it, why do you boast as if you did not receive it? *(I Corinthians 4:7b)*

Whatever you do, work heartily, as for the Lord and not for men, knowing that from the Lord you will receive the inheritance as your reward. You are serving the Lord Christ.

(Colossians 3:23-24)

As each has received a gift, use it to serve one another, as good stewards of God's varied grace: whoever speaks, as one who speaks oracles of God; whoever serves, as one who serves by the strength that God supplies—in order that in everything God may be glorified through Jesus Christ. To him belong glory and dominion forever and ever. Amen. *(I Peter 4:10-11)*

See also—Genesis 1:27, Psalm 139:14, Matthew 7:11, James 1:17, Matthew 25:21

A Vision of Value

"In the image of God" He created me;
I am "fearfully, wonderfully made."
Yet I've sought for approval from all I see:
A life spent being measured and weighed.

Then, each day I have judged my own worth to give
An opinion too high or too low.
Is this truly the way I'm designed to live?
In God's Word is the answer I know:

"Do not fear; I've redeemed you, and you are Mine,"
Says my God, "I have called you by name."
Thus, when God looks at me, He sees His design:
One He formed—one for whom Jesus came.

Jesus said, "Before men you must shine your light—
Your good works they will see and accord
All the glory to God. This is just and right;
He's the Source of all blessings outpoured."

For just what is my light? Does it come from me?
It's each talent and gift, every skill
Which "the Father of lights" makes and grants so free
In accord with His purpose and will.

Nothing good is in me that I've not received:
I can't boast of what isn't my own.
And my worth's not increased by what I've achieved,
For it's all to God's glory alone.

Thus, I'm free now to labor with all my heart,
Not for self, not for men—for the Lord,
Since my worth and my work have been pried apart,
And from Christ I'll receive my reward.

So, I'll use what I'm given to serve each one
As a steward of "God's varied grace,"
Wanting only to hear Jesus say, "Well done"
When I see the pure light of His face!

Through [Christ] we have also obtained access by faith into this grace in which we stand, and we rejoice in hope of the glory of God.   *(Romans 5:2)*

And my God will supply every need of yours according to his riches in glory in Christ Jesus.   *(Philippians 4:19)*

For in [Christ] the whole fullness of deity dwells bodily, and you have been filled in him, who is the head of all rule and authority.   *(Colossians 2:9-10)*

For from him and through him and to him are all things. To him be glory forever. Amen.   *(Romans 11:36)*

Prayers of Petition and Praise
(adapted from Ephesians 1:17-20, 3:14-21)

The Apostle Paul wrote great letters that taught
Of the grace that the Savior's spilled blood dearly bought.
Then he gave instructions and warned of sin's snares,
But he poured out his heart for the saints in his prayers:

"I entreat the God of our Lord Jesus Christ—
He's the Father of glory whose Son sacrificed.
May He give a spirit of wisdom to you,
Revelation that brings His true nature in view,
That you'd have the eyes of your heart with light filled
So you'll know what's the hope of the calling He willed,
Know the glorious riches of those set apart:
You, the saints—the inheritance dear to God's heart;
And know, too, how great is His unsurpassed might
That's for us who believe and receive Jesus' light.
That same pow'r raised Christ from the grave to God's hand—
All of these are the things I pray you'll understand!

"And I bow my knees to the Father and claim
That from Him every family on earth gets its name.
I then ask that He'd truly grant, in accord
With the wealth that His riches in glory afford,
That you'd thus be strengthened with power inside
Through His Spirit who brings all that God has supplied,
So that Christ, through faith, in your hearts may dwell;
And that you, being grounded in love, now, as well,
May have strength to then, with the saints, comprehend
What's the breadth and the length, height and depth without end,
And to know Christ's love that's beyond all we know.
Thus, you're filled with the fullness of God's overflow!"

Paul concludes his prayer of petition with praise,
A doxology that should resound all our days:
"Now to Him who's able to do so much more
Than all things we might ask or could think are in store,
By the pow'r we see that is working within,
Yes, to Him be the glory in the church, also, in
Jesus Christ through all generations, and then
For forever and ever and ever. Amen."